Fr. Slavko Barbarić, O.F.M.

PRAY WITH THE HEART!

Međugorje Manual of Prayer

MEDUGORJE

In accordance with the decree of Pope Urban VIII and Act II of the Vatican Council, the writer states that he does not question church authority, to which he submits completely. The words »apparitions, miracles, messages« and others used in this book have the value of human testimony.

English translation: Jozo Kraljević

Published by: Parish Office
88266 Medugorje

Printed in Yugoslavia by:
»Grafotisak«, Grude

Published in the United States by
Franciscan University Press
Steubenville, OH 43952
ISBN 0-940535-34-3

TABLE OF CONTENTS

INTRODUCTION

Unusual as it may sound, it is at the same time true, our time is a praying time. The people of our time, who are always in a hurry, stop to pray after all. They do so because they feel a primeval need to talk to God, to tell him what they are unable to tell another person, not even the closest of friends. For people know that God is the closest and most intimate friend a person can have, after all.

Therefore, dear readers, if you want to be close to and more intimate with our greatest friend, Jesus Christ, then stop and reflect on this book. It will teach you, in a simple way, how to love God and your neighbor, without which love, prayer cannot be fruitful.

This book does not threaten. It does not speak about God's punishment, but about God's love. It calls to us and upon us to be the proud and devout children of God. It calls us, the small, to become great by following Jesus' Gospel. It calls us, who are weary and burdened, to find rest and peace through the power of Jesus' Gospel. It calls us sinners to become holy through Jesus' Gospel.

We have read many books about prayer. But finally, here is a book which is itself a prayer. This book does not deal with how it should be prayed, but it is prayed as every Christian believer should pray - from heart to heart, from soul to soul, and from the painful cry of a miserable man to the merciful response of the God-man.

Rivers and streams of grace flow between us. Year after year. Day after day. Shall we bypass these rivers and streams? Shall we allow these living waters, the waters of mercy, to flow away into the immense abyss of hopelessness? Of course, we are not going to allow something like that. And it is exactly this wonderful spiritual book of the spiritual scientist, Fr. Slavko Barbarić, O.F.M., Ph.D., which, in a wonderful and simple way, speaks of all the beauties of Christian spirituality.

Whoever has read this book, will truly enrich himself spiritually. Whoever accepts this book as a prayer manual, will discover the best prayerbook. And he who accepts it merely as a literary form, will not be disappointed either.

Jakov Bubalo

PRACTICAL INSTRUCTIONS

Morning and Evening Prayers

Beginners can select everyday one of the seven points of the prayer pattern which ends with one Our Father, Hail Mary, Glory Be and the Creed.

Those who feel a greater need of meeting God in prayer will select one of the seven suggested patterns and recite seven Our Fathers, Hail Marys, and Glory Bes, and the Creed.

The most advanced will find time to go through all seven points everyday or at least once a week.

Adoration of the Most Blessed Sacrament

Adoration of the Most Blessed Sacrament has been practiced in Medugorje since 1982, first on the first Thursday in the month and then, since March 1, 1984, on every Thursday, after the evening Mass. Groups and individuals can make use of this pattern in their churches whenever they want to. But for everyday visits to Jesus, one point of meditation can suffice.

Adoration of the Cross

This devotion has been customary in the Međugorje church since 1984, on Fridays after evening Mass. Elsewhere it can be made according to need, especially during Lent. Its parts, as independent wholes, can also be used individually in everyday life. They are especially recommended to the sick and their attendants.

The Way of the Cross

While you are in Međugorje, you will best experience the Way of the Cross by climbing Mount Križevac. Likewise, you can make this devotion in any church or chapel, or in your room on Fridays and whenever you want to experience Jesus' Easter message about the meaning of His suffering.

Prayers for Healing

Prayers for healing are regularly said in Međugorje after the evening Mass. They can be used by all who want to pray for healing, depending on their needs.

Praying the Rosary

Since August 1984, the whole Rosary has been recited daily in Međugorje: two parts before Mass, and the third part after Mass. If you cannot pray the whole Rosary everyday, then, according to the common practice in the Church, pray the Joyful Mysteries on Mondays and Thursdays, the Sorrowful Mysteries on Tuesdays and Fridays, and the Glorious Mysteries on Wednesdays, Saturdays and Sundays.

The Rosary of Peace and the Jesus Rosary can be prayed according to one's own disposition.

Preface

When you come to Međugorje, you will hear that we are called to prayer. We are called not only to prayer in the morning or evening, to individual or common prayer, but to prayer with the heart as well.

Every prayer can be finished in haste so that we say all our prayers to the end, without having met Jesus and Mary. If we continue on like this, there is a danger of our having only wasted our time and never coming to like prayer. Therefore, it is important to find time for prayer.

In this booklet you will find that Our Lady invites you to prayer in front of the cross, and to prayer in front of the Most Blessed Sacrament. She also invites you to confess properly, to prepare yourself properly for Holy Mass and to give thanks after it. You will find messages urging you to devote yourself to God through the Virgin Mary. To devote oneself to God means to decide everyday for love, for forgiving, for charity, and against evil and sin, against Satan and all his deeds, as well as against all collaboration with him.

These are the principal thoughts that will lead us through this prayer booklet.

I would certainly like this book to be only an incentive. The prayers which follow are the result of an experience. This prayer manual will serve its purpose if it helps you to formulate your own personal prayer which will include the same elements.

With the messages which Our Lady gives, formerly on Thursdays and now on the 25th of every month, she has offered us her life of prayer and shows us how to grow spiritually.

Everything is directed to the person of Jesus Christ. Our Lady is aware that all her qualities result only from her personal relationship with Jesus Christ. And everything she has advised us has only one aim, to bring us to Jesus.

And to come to Jesus means to touch the source of life which gives the water that never runs dry. For Jesus is the model of a man who is at the same time God as well.

These prayers have been woven from a praying experience and have matured with the messages. May they help you, too, dear pilgrim, to come a step closer to Jesus. He will bring you closer to peace, to love, to reconciliation and togetherness of all people as brothers and sisters, to the growing together of God's people into a large family. And exactly such a family gathers in Medugorje from all the four winds, where »Christ is its head, the Holy Spirit its strength, Mary its mother, and heaven its home.«

Only in this way shall we be able to experience how good it is to be together like brothers and sisters, gathered around the same Mother, who leads on and does not stop leading until we all come to our Father's home.

Dear pilgrim, may your coming to Medugorje be a step closer to all this and finally a preparation for a safe passage to our eternal homeland!

The Places of Prayer in Međugorje

The apparitions started on Podbrdo, known today as the Hill of Apparitions. Through the force of circumstances they were transferred to houses, then to the parish church, to the rectory, to the choir loft in the church, and finally to wherever the visionaries are. From time to time the apparitions occurred on Mount Križevac as well.

When the restrictions on movement about the parish at the time of Our Lady's apparitions were lifted, the bud of Međugorje started to develop into a beautiful flower. Now, the overall experience of Međugorje for most pilgrims includes not only the evening service in the parish church, but also the penitential ascent of the Hill of Apparitions above Bijakovići, and of Mt. Križevac, above Međugorje. These three places of prayer certainly form part of the outward spiritual program as well.

Therefore, when you come to Međugorje, alone or in a group, go into the church and pray. That is the beginning. Pay homage to Jesus. Open your heart to Him completely. If you can, go to confession. Start your pilgrim day here. Take part in the Mass of your language group. Give thanks after Mass. This is the first step you can take in Međugorje, to pray in the church and to meet Jesus like the shepherds in Bethlehem did.

From church, if you can, start for Križevac. It is best to set out on foot from the church. No matter whether you go alone or in a group, start praying immediately. It is like the road from Bethlehem to Calvary. When you start climbing up the mountain itself, the Stations of the Cross wait for you. Stop at each and think. In this booklet you will find enough help for it. Take your time, do not hurry. Unite yourself with Jesus. When you reach the top, pray under the Cross, be the weather nice or bad. Take courage. Pray your fullest under the Cross. Cry your heart out because of your sins. Open your heart before the Cross and you will know what it means. In this booklet you will also find a prayer of adoration before the Cross. Pray. Never mind the time. Whoever perseveres under the Cross, can go further, receive new assignments and have new experiences.

The view from the Cross opens wide in all directions. Especially, it opens towards the Hill of Apparitions, towards Podbrdo. Go to this place, too, and pray. It is not as steep as Križevac, as Calvary, but it is a hill nevertheless. We have become used to learning about meetings on hills from Jesus' life. Before His Ascension to heaven, He called His disciples together on a hill and then sent them to Jerusalem to pray and from there, to the whole world. Open your heart again on the Hill of Apparitions. Here you will sense, in a special way, how resurrection is close to us, how a road into the world opens to us, waiting for us, full of troubles and hardships. Mary appeared on this Hill, first with a child in her arms, then with the Cross. From this hill, many have gone home and started doing whatever the Lord told them.

If you stay for several days, dear pilgrim, go again to each mountain. Each time is a new experience.

Do not look for the visionaries, do not bother about shopping. Try to live humbly. Mary educates for new simplicity. But without Bethlehem, without the Cross, without the meeting on the Hill of Mission and without Jerusalem, as places of prayer, we cannot understand what is essential in Medugorje, nor can we be sent out.

MORNING PRAYER

1. In the name of the Father, and of the Son, and of the Holy Spirit do I begin this day. Father, thank you for having created me with the characteristics of spirit and body.

Thank you for having created time, which flows and empties into eternity. Thank you for eternity, which does not pass away. Thank you for immersing me into your immense love and for my enjoying an untroubled bliss forever. Thank you for the hope that awakens in me again this morning, for it is going to be my strength for this day, with all its troubles, sufferings and problems. I know that nothing is vain for those who are with you, who seek you in everything.

Thank you for the light of this new day, for it helps me to imagine the eternal light that never sets. Therefore, I open myself to the created light in order to attain the uncreated and eternal light.

Father, thank you for having sent us your Son Jesus Christ who said of himself: »I am the Light of the world, I am the Way for the world, I am the Truth of the world.«

Father, thank you for your Spirit, by whose help I shall be able to live in the light today, to make progress on the way and to live the truth.

This morning, Father, I also thank you for Mother Mary. She is the lodestar of the new day, the dawn of a new daybreak, a mother clothed with the sun, with the moon at her feet. You showed in her what you offer to us all. Thank you for having created her without sin in the bosom of her mother and for having prepared her immaculate heart as the first abode for your Son in the Holy Spirit.

Father, grant that I may start this day with joy, in the light of your love. Grant that I may understand it as your gift. Help me to live joyfully in hope. Give me a joyful strength for love, for good deeds, for reconciliation, and a permanent longing for you, the spring of pure joy.

(Remain in silence. After a short meditation confide your plans and duties of this day to the Lord.)

Our Father, Hail Mary, Glory Be...

2. Father, thank you for my being able today to decide for you in all my thoughts, feelings and actions. Now, too, I decide for

you as your Son Jesus Christ decided for you and as His and our Mother decided for you. She invited me, too, in your name with the following words:

»Dear children: I call upon you to decide for God completely. I beg you, dear children, to abandon yourselves completely to God and you will be able to live all that I am talking about. It will not be difficult for you to surrender to God completely. Thank you for having responded to my call« (January 2, 1986).

Father, I decide for you, and pray to you that my decision may be permanent, that you may, also today, have the first place for me in every situation, that I may also today seek your glory and live in your love. I pray especially to you that I may withstand all the trials of the day. Do not allow my love and my devotion to be weak.

I pray to you, Lord, for those I will meet today that they will decide to live for you devotedly. Then my devotion will be easier, too. May my devotion and my decision this morning be a support and an encouragement to others.

(Recommend by name those whom you know you are going to meet today.)

Our Father, Hail Mary, Glory Be...

3. Father, thank you that by my decision and devotion I belong to you today and forever. I know, Father, that both in me and in the world there is still a lot of evil and sin. I know that the Prince of Darkness, the archenemy of men from the beginning, the Seducer and the Deceiver, Satan, is not idle but seduces and destroys love and peace. Therefore, now, at the beginning of this day, I consciously decide for you, and against Satan. I renounce all his seductions. I break off every collaboration with him.

Father, thank you for having given me freedom and for my being able to decide for you of my own free will. Thank you that your Son and our Savior Jesus exposed the action of evil and conquered it by the strength of his love and sacrifice. Thank you, Father, not only for having preserved Mary from sin and the effect of evil, but also for having made her our mighty intercessor.

Mary, this morning I want to respond to the call which you address to all:

»**Dear children: I invite each of you to start living in God's love. Dear children, you are ready to commit sin, and to give yourselves up into the hands of Satan thoughtlessly. I invite each of you to de-**

cide for God consciously, and against Satan. I am your mother. Therefore, I want to lead you all to complete holiness. I want each of you to be with me in heaven. This is, dear children, the purpose of my coming here, and my wish. Thank you for having responded to my call« (May 25, 1987).

Mary, this morning I really want to respond to your call. I am sorry that I am still inclined to commit sin, that I still do not love as I should, that there are still moments when earthly things are more important to me than the spiritual ones. I am sorry that my words are not always very kind, that my thoughts are sometimes unchaste.

I do not want to sin any more. I renounce sin. I renounce every unconscious collaboration with evil. If there is anything left in me that serves sin and that gives me up thoughtlessly into the hands of the enemy of my spirit, soul and body, the enemy of my life, now I renounce it deliberately. With you, O Mary, I pray for the favor of being aware of all my actions, that all my actions may be in the service of goodness, love, peace and reconciliation.

(Think of your evil habits and sins and renounce them quite concretely, mentioning them by name.)

Our Father, Hail Mary, Glory Be...

4. Father, you created me in such a way as to be able, only through my love for you and my neighbors, to become happy here on earth and come into heavenly, eternal happiness. Therefore, I renounce every dislike, every hatred, all bad ways, every blasphemy, either of mine or of others, and decide for LOVE. Send me your Spirit that I may love you as your Son Jesus Christ loved

you. Give me love that I may love you in all men and in all creatures. Thank you that your Son Jesus Christ gave his life for me out of love. That is why today, in spite of all my sins, I cry for joy: »Father, I want to love you.«

Thank you for having made Mary, the Mother, a mother of goodness, love and mercy. Thank you that she wants to educate us for love towards you and towards all men.

Mary, thank you for being so tireless in the effort to teach us love. Thank you for this call:

»Dear children, today I invite you to live the words I LOVE GOD this week. Dear children, by love you shall achieve everything, even what you think impossible. God wants this parish to belong completely to Him. And that is what I want, too. Thank you for having responded to my call« (February 28, 1985).

Mary, at your motherly word I decide that I shall live love for God every moment of this day. O Mother of love, teach me love and pray for love with me.

Mary, I pray to you now for all those I will work with and live with today that they may live your message as well. Let my decision be a help to them, as their decision will help me.

(Mention by name those you will meet, those you work with and those you work for, that there may be love in everything.)

Our Father, Hail Mary, Glory Be...

5. Father, you wanted me to be born into a family, too. At the beginning of this day I thank you for my family, for every member of family, my close and my distant relatives. Without them I would be lonesome and forsaken. My life would not be orderly and work would not be possible for me. There-

fore, Father, thank you for their love towards me, because it comes from you. Thank you for all the good and nice things I have experienced in my family and with my dear ones.

(Mention them by name.)

I decide personally for love in my family and I would like to love them all as you love us all. I also pray to you for the families of my brothers and sisters, of all my relatives, and for all families in the world. Father, to your love I commend all those who have remained without love and peace, because sin has destroyed them. Give them back the strength for love and peace. Heal their wounds. Make them happy.

Mary, Mother of our families, thank you for having lived in the holy family and for having shown that it is possible to live in togetherness and with love. Intercede for us and pray for our families. Thank you for being our teacher in this message as well:

»Dear children: you know that the time of joy is approaching, and without love you will achieve nothing. Therefore, first start loving your family, all your parishioners, and then you will be able to accept and love all those who come here. Let this week be a time for you to learn how to

love. Thank you for having responded to my call« (December 13, 1984).

Refresh me personally and protect my decisions with your motherly mantle. Grant that today in my family love may be the principal rule of behavior between each other. Let love, through your intercession, heal all wounds from yesterday, and let joy make its abode in us.

Our Father, Hail Mary, Glory Be...

6. Father, this morning I thank you especially for the grace to cooperate in building the world with the gifts you have given me. Ahead of me is a day given as gift by your grace. I want to do everything for your glory, for my own good and for the good of all people. Teach me so that my work today will be a continuation of this morning's prayer.

Bless my family at work, the community and the whole world. Bless all those who work today, but also those who do not work because they are unemployed or do not know how to find employment. Hire them all in your vineyard to build a better world. Do not allow us to overwork. Refresh the tired, inspire the artists, open to inventors an approach to new discoveries of the laws you put into your creation. Grant that everything may praise and glorify you.

You, Father, sent your Son to teach us how to work. All He did was for your greater glory. Let Him enrich us with His Spirit that we may keep the balance between manual labor and mental work.

Mary, our Mother, thank you for having called us to turn to the Creator in our work and to ask His blessing before and after our work.

»Dear children. Today I want to tell you to pray before starting to work and to finish your work with prayer. If you do so, God will bless both you and your work. These days you have been praying little and working much. So pray. You will find rest in prayer. Thank you for having responded to my call« (July 5, 1984).

Thank you for your motherly call. Mother Mary, pray with me to the Father that He may forgive me for having so many times forgotten to ask for His fatherly blessing. May He forgive me for having often considered myself as the master, forgetting that I am only the administrator of the goods entrusted to me, and for having so often misused my working abilities. Mother, let me become a good cooperator with God's plans. Mary, pray to the Father that He may forgive all for having sometimes destroyed themselves both with overwork and idleness. Let all people consciously and joyfully work together in building the world, and let everybody's work today be blessed.

Our Father, Hail Mary, Glory Be...

7. Father, now in this prayer I have opened my heart before you and nourished my soul to the full. Refresh both my soul and body that I may be able to fulfill my tasks. Here I am, Father. I repeat this word with your Son Jesus Christ for all the nice and hard moments that lie in store for me today. I pronounce the words that Mary, the Mother of your son said: »I am the servant of the Lord.«

Mary, thank you for helping me to understand that I am also important for the salvation of the world; that I, too, can bring peace and love.

»**Dear children: I invite you to be an example to others in everything, especially in prayer and in testifying. Dear children, I cannot help the world without you. I want you to cooperate with me in everything, even in the least things. So, dear children, help me that your prayer may come from the heart and that you all may give yourselves up to me completely. In this way I shall be with you. Thank you**

for having responded to my call« (August 28, 1986).

The servant of God, I am ready to respond and come with you to help the world. Thank you that want to be with me and that I am important to you. Thank you for the words that you cannot help the world without me. Let me understand, like you did, the Father's plan for me today. Amen.

Our Father, Hail Mary, Glory Be...

Trusting in you, Father, I repeat with the Church that I believe in you and that I confide my heart to you.

I believe in God . .

EVENING PRAYER

1. Father, the day has passed and the evening has come. I pray to you to send me your Spirit that I may, in your light, consciously spend these moments which I want to dedicate to you and to myself. Thank you for being ready to listen to me as your child.

Father, hush my heart as the heart of a child is hushed in its father's arms. Hush my heart at the sunset of this day as a baby is hushed in its mother's bosom. As everything around me is falling into the darkness of the night, send me your light which never passes. Appease my soul as a doe is appeased at a water spring and as the earth is appeased after a fruitful rain.

Mary, so many times you hushed Jesus, your Son, as a child in your motherly bosom and committed Him to the calm of the night. So I, too, ask you to be with me in these moments, that peace and tranquillity may enter into my heart, that they may affect my soul and body.

Mary, thank you for having called me to change my heart. You said:

»Dear children: I would like to tell you today to start working on your hearts like you work in your fields. Work and change

your hearts that a new spirit from God may settle down in them. Thank you for having responded to my call« (April 25, 1985).

(Remain in silence and open to peace.)

Our Father, Hail Mary, Glory Be...

2. Father, I have worked today and have become tired. Thank you for my having had a chance to make use of the gifts you gave me for my own good and for the good of others. Thank you that I have worked hard today, too. And now I pray to you to give me grace to cultivate my heart, as I was ready to do other jobs during the day. Father, I pray to you that I may, at Mary's intercession, redecorate and cultivate my heart, that it may change and become good and pure. Remove from it the dust of sin and evil. Let a new Spirit make its abode in me. Father, I admit that I have sinned today, too. At times selfishness and haughtiness took hold of me. I was angry and impatient. Others around me have sinned, too, uttering blasphemies, curses, lies and slanders. Father, all this has burdened my heart. So, cleanse and wash me. Cleanse my consciousness and subconsciousness that peace may settle down in me.

Mary, thank you for your call to cleanse ourselves of sin:

»**Dear children: Today, too, I invite you to prepare your hearts for all the days when the Lord especially wants to cleanse you of all sins from your past. You, dear children, are not able to do it alone. That is why I am here to help you. Pray, dear children. Only in this way will you be able to recognize all the evil that is in you and to deliver it to the Lord in order that He may completely cleanse your hearts. So, dear children, pray without ceasing and prepare your hearts in penance and fasting. Thank you for having responded to my call«** (December 4, 1986).

Mary, thank you for being here to help us to cleanse ourselves. O Mother, take me on your lap now. A mother makes little of how much her child is dirty and soiled, she rather helps it to be clean and nice. Do so with me now. Let the Lord, at your intercession, take the burdens from my heart.

(Remain again in silence.)

Our Father, Hail Mary, Glory Be...

3. Father, now I pray to you for my family.

(Mention the members of your family or the members of your community by name.)

Let none of us go to the night's rest, burdened with the sins of the day. You know us well. Thank you for not condemning us but for giving us also, at the end of this day, the grace to cleanse ourselves and so to be able to meet tomorrow and work together for your glory. Heal the wounds we have inflicted on each other by insufficient love, mistrust, or slander. Father, cleanse and calm each one of us that peace may flourish tomorrow.

(Pray especially for the person you may have quarreled and argued with, who hurt you and left a wound in you. Do this in silence.)

Mary, through your motherly intercession, help my family and my community. Help all families to enjoy the night's peace with you in the Lord. Mary, thank you for the words with which you called us to inner beauty, when you said:

»**Dear children: I want to invite you again to prayer today. When praying you are much more beautiful, like flowers which after snow, show all their beauty and all their colors become indescribable. Likewise, dear children, after prayer you**

show to better advantage before God, all your good points, which makes you dear to Him. So, dear children, pray and open your inner self to the Lord that He may make you an harmonious and beautiful flowerforheaven. Thank you for having responded tomycall« (December 18, 1986).

Mary, Mother of goodness, love and mercy, Mother full of divine beauty, let our family become a new wonderful flower. Let the ice of misunderstanding disappear from our family and from all families. Let everybody open and confide his inner self to you, like a child confides in its mother. Mary, thank you for being ready to be our mother, although many times we have refused to cooperate with your calls. From now on we want to be beautiful and show the beauty of all the colors given to us. Grant that we may become endeared to each other, and, all together with you, to the Lord.

Our Father, Hail Mary, Glory Be...

4. Father, thank you for giving me back my peace, for healing my wounds and the wounds of my family. Thank you for delivering me from the burden of the day that I may immerse myself into a deep peace and regain strength for the new day and for new cooperation with you in the world. But

before I close my eyes, my thoughts go also to those of your children, my brothers and sisters, who cannot have a peaceful sleep because they are burdened. Therefore, I pray to you with Mary, the Mother of your Son and the Mother of us all, that they may find peace, too. You know that hatred breaks families and communities, so that many are on the streets now, abandoned, despised, seeking consolation in alcohol and drugs, and in a dissipated life. But peace they do not find, nor is consolation given to them. Only new wounds are opened and a new grief reigns in hearts and families. Father, I pray to you for them. I especially include the young, the children who do not find rest nor repose because their parents are at odds with each other. Mary, I pray for them together with you, for you said:

»Dear children: I invite you again to prayer with the heart. If you pray with your heart, dear children, the ice cold hearts of your brothers will melt and all obstacles will disappear. Conversion will be easy for all those who want to receive it. It is a gift you have to obtain by prayer for your neighbor. Thank you for having responded to my call« (January 23, 1986).

Mary, all men are my neighbors. So, at your word I pray to the Lord that all obstacles to peace and tranquillity may disappear. May all be converted and saved. Let the spring of joy and togetherness come to all men.

(Recommend in silence somebody whom you know is in restlessness and anxiety.)

Our Father, Hail Mary, Glory Be...

5. Father, now I direct my thoughts to those who cannot enter into a peaceful sleep and who do not find appeasement in their heart, because they are weighed down with illness or because they attend the sick. I pray to you with an honest heart for them, too.

Look upon all the sick in our families and in our hospitals. Who can appease and soothe their heart if not you, Lord of all hearts? Alleviate their wounds and pains. Give them love that they can bear their pains, like your Son bore His cross. Father, I pray to you for your sick children and my sick brothers and sisters. Grant your grace to all who suffer from mental or physical pains that they may present their crosses for their own salvation and the salvation of the world. In this moment, let them also know that you accept their sacrifices.

Bless especially those who nurse the sick. Let their love for the sick be inexhaustible. Send them rest and peace by the gift of love that comes from you.

Mary, faithful Mother, you did not run away from the cross of your Son but remained loyal to the end. Let all those who cannot find a peaceful rest now feel that you are with them. Obtain grace for them through prayer that they may offer their sacrifices to God, as you called us all:

»Dear children: I thank you for every sacrifice you have offered. I again urge you to offer each sacrifice with love. I want you, the helpless, to start helping with confidence, and the Lord will give to you in confidence. Thank you for having responded to my call« (July 4, 1985).

Mary, thank you for these words. Let them echo in the hearts of all the sick and infirm, of all who suffer in one way or another. Mother of consolation, obtain grace for them by prayer that they may understand with the heart this word of yours and constantly offer themselves as a living sacrifice of love for salvation. You know how pain and suffering can exhaust and take away all inner strength. So obtain, through your prayers, peace and tranquillity for them.

(Recommend especially a sick person you know.)

Our Father, Hail Mary, Glory Be...

6. Father, I cannot go to my sleep without praying to you, sincerely and from my heart, for all those who are at war now, who persecute and destroy each other with modern weapons. Father, forgive us for having misused our achievements, and the laws you have allowed us to discover, to make weapons and other means of destruction. You wanted them to serve us for good. Father, forgive our wars and conflicts. Heal the hearts of all who are deceived and exploited, who are persecuted and deprived of their rights, that peace may come to a world which thirsts after it.

Father, give back peace to those who in their hearts bear the need for violence and revenge. Open the way of peace to every heart. Send them your light to make them aware of all lies and deceit so that nobody ever becomes a victim of their violence again.

Enlighten with your light all statesmen, all parliaments, all those who make decisions about the destiny of the world. Let them bow down before you. Let them recognize you as the Lord. Let them work for peace. Let them understand that all authority is given from you as a gift for service. Father, let us understand that peace is not for us only nor for our friends, but for all people. O, let peace come.

Mary, Queen and Mother of Peace, obtain through prayers, peace for each of your children and for each family. At your word I pray now before the cross for peace, for you said:

»Dear children: There is no peace without prayer. So I tell you, dear children, to pray for peace in front of the cross. Thank you for having responded to my call« (September 6, 1984).

(Remain kneeling for a while in front of the cross and mention the unreconciled. Then pray.)

Our Father, Hail Mary, Glory Be...

7. Father, at the end of my prayer this evening I ask you for your blessing. Bless me with the blessing of peace, love and reconciliation. Bless me that I may grow while my body is at rest. Bless me that my love may be alive while my body and soul are overcome by sleep. Let the seed of your word grow in me through your blessing,

while I am asleep. Let it grow irrepressibly both in my family and in the whole world.

Mary, Mother of goodness and love, Mother of God's Word, be with me and with every one of your children. Drive away every evil and every influence of evil from me and from all people. Obtain by prayer, together with me, the blessing you invited us all to when you said:

»Dear children: I would like to invite you to grow in love. A flower cannot grow normally without water. Neither can you, dear children, grow without God's blessing. You should seek God's blessing from day to day so that you may grow normally and do everything with God. Thank you for having responded to my call« (April 10, 1986).

Here, Mary, I am asking for a blessing with you. Obtain it from God, in all its fullness, by prayer for me.

Our Father, Hail Mary, Glory Be...

Father, at the end I give my heart over to you and pray, confess my faith in you, the Triune God, Father, Son and Holy Spirit.

I believe ...

PRAYER TO THE HOLY SPIRIT

Mary, thank you for having called me to pray everyday to the Holy Spirit through whom you conceived Jesus Christ, through whom you, in meditation, understood the Word of God and remained faithful to it to the end.

»Dear children: This evening I would like to tell you to pray in the days of this Novena for the outpouring of the Holy Spirit on your families and on your parish. Pray. You shall not regret it. God shall give you the gifts with which you will praise Him to the last breath of your life on earth. Thank you for having responded to my call« (June 2, 1984).

O Spirit, I pray to you now with Mary who called me to pray to you. Pour yourself out on me with all your gifts.

Pour out the gift of love into my life that from now on I may love God in you above all, and my neighbor as myself.

Pour out on me the gift of wisdom that in everything I do, think, feel and decide, I may always think, decide and act in your light.

O Spirit of Counsel, descend on me that I may, with my knowledge and the word of love, help those who ask me for counsel. Let my every word be a light to others.

Spirit of Jesus, grant me the gift of your strength that I may stand every trial and do the Father's will, especially in times of hardship. Spirit of fortitude, strengthen me in the hours of frailty.

O Spirit of life, develop the divine life which was given to me, through you, when I was in the bosom of my mother and again at my baptism.

Divine fire, inflame the fire of divine love in my heart so that the darkness and ice of sin may disappear from it.

Spirit of healing, heal within me all that is wounded and develop the undeveloped.

Descend on me with all your strength that I may be thankful for small things as well. Enlighten me, Holy Spirit, that I may know how to appreciate crosses and hardships, too.

Mary, you are the bearer of the Holy Spirit. Thank you for calling me to pray to the Spirit of truth:

»Dear children: Tomorrow evening pray for the Spirit of truth. Especially you from the parish, for you need the Spirit of truth that you convey the messages as

they are, without adding to or taking away anything from them, just the way I put them. Pray that the Holy Spirit may inspire you with the spirit of prayer, that you may pray more. I, your Mother, tell you that you pray little. Thank you for having responded to my call« (June 9, 1984).

O Spirit of truth, enlighten me with your truth that I may first live the truth of love, peace and righteousness. Help me that I may be able, with my words and deeds, to proclaim every day the Word of the Father in its full light, to everybody.

Holy Spirit, guide our Pope, bishops, priests and all others who proclaim the Word of God. Fall on the parish community of Medugorje, too, that it may be able to live Our Lady's messages and convey them to all. Fall on the priests who preach in Medugorje. Fall on the confessors and those who confess.

Spirit of prayer, teach us how to pray. Cleanse our hearts that we may pray worthily and always find time for prayer. Holy Spirit, pray within me and invoke Abba, Father. Grant me the favor of praying with the heart.

Mary, I also want to open my heart to the Holy Spirit, as you opened yours when you called me:

»Dear children: These days I invite you especially to open your hearts to the Holy Spirit. These days the Holy Spirit acts through you in a special way. Open your hearts and abandon your life to Jesus that He may act through your hearts and strengthen your faith. Thank you for having responded to my call« (May 23, 1985).

Holy Spirit, take away all burdens from me that my heart may be like a developing and growing flower that brings abundant fruit. Mary, may the Holy Spirit start and continue within me the deed which started in you, that the divine Word may grow within me.

O Holy Spirit, through Mary I choose you today as the Master of my whole being. With trust and hope in your endless love, which manifested itself so marvelously in Mary, I decide for your gifts. I renounce every evil spirit and his action, and accept you, Spirit of light, love, peace and order. I dedicate to you all my abilities and want to act in your light. I surrender to you all rights over my life. Watch over me and lead me to the

Father. I pray to you with Mary through Jesus Christ. Amen.

PRAYER OF CONSECRATION TO OUR LADY
(To be prayed especially on Our Lady's feasts)

»Dear children: Today again I invite you to devote your life to me with love that I may be able to lead you with love. I love you, dear children, with a special love and I want to bring you all to heaven, to God. I want you to understand that this life is so short compared to that one in heaven. So, dear children, decide for God again today. Only then shall I be able to show you how dear you are to me and how much I wish you were all saved and in heaven with me. Thank you for having responded to my call« (November 27, 1986).

Mary, thank you for this motherly call. Mother of my Savior and Mother of Peace, today I surrender my life to you with love. As Jesus, dying on the cross, gave you to me, so do I give myself to you now. Take me on your motherly lap. I want to love Jesus as you did, Mother. I want to learn with you how to listen to the Father's word and do his will.

Mary, with you I wish to learn how to love all people as my brothers and sisters because they are all yours. I devote myself to you that my prayer may be the prayer of the heart in which I shall find peace, and love, and the strength of reconciliation. To you, O Lady, do I give up my past, my present and my future, and all my abilities and gifts. I want to grow up with you like Jesus did. Let everything in me praise the Lord with you. And from now on, let my soul sing for joy for His love and mercy. I dedicate to you, Mother, my family, too, all my friends, all those I live with and those I work with.

Mary, I would like to be the bearer of the Holy Spirit with you. Let my heart be obedient to His inspirations, as was yours.

Mother of Peace, let my words be irrevocable through your intercession that sin may never seduce me again. Amen.

PRAYING THE ROSARY

In all her apparitions, Our Lady has called us to prayer. She did not ask for new forms of prayer, nor did she offer them. She rather asked for old forms to be renewed and to be given a new life force.

Such is the case with Medugorje, too. At the beginning she suggested seven Our Fathers, Hail Marys, and Glory Bes, and the Creed as the minimum of daily prayer. Then she called for one part of the Rosary and finally for all three parts. On the eve of the great feast of her Assumption, August 14, 1984, Our Lady said through Ivan Dragičević:

»I would like the world to pray with me these days. As much as possible, to fast on Wednesdays and Fridays, and to pray at least the Rosary every day; joyful, sorrowful and glorious mysteries...«

Meaning of the Rosary

To pray the Rosary means nothing else than to find a way to be with Jesus and Mary.

By meditating on the mysteries of their life, we are with Jesus and Mary: be it the joy of Christmas and the seriousness of the presentation in the temple, or the sorrow and bloody sweat on His face, the wounds on His back from the scourge and the cross, or the crown of thorns on His head. When we are daily linked with Mary and Jesus by such meetings, then the joy of victory over death and sin is guaranteed to us with them and the gifts of the Spirit and the final triumph in heaven are assured us.

So, to recite the Rosary does not mean to hide oneself somewhere in a corner and to live far from the world and life. It means to prepare oneself for one's own and other people's crosses, the way Jesus and Mary carried them. To be with them means to have troubles and problems, and yet never to become embittered. To be with them means to experience contempt and disappointment, and yet never to seek for revenge. To go with them means to go the way of a person who believes in God who makes everything new.

Every prayer can be finished in a hasty manner so that we »say« all our prayers to the end without having met Jesus and Mary. If we do this, there is danger that prayer will become a waste of time for us and we will never come to like prayer. It is just like meeting a friend. If we never have time for our friend or, if the time we devote to him is too short, of if we speak with bad grace, then the friendship is bound to die.

Therefore, it is important to have time for the prayer of the Rosary and for every prayer.

In this book, you will find the prayer of the Rosary (Joyful, Sorrowful and Glorious mysteries) with Biblical texts and some personal prayers. Then we give an example of the Rosary for Peace and of the Jesus Rosary.

Before starting to pray, remember Our Lady's messages about the Rosary. Here are some of them:

»Dear children. Today I would like to ask you to make me happy with your prayers again and again. Unfortunately there are a lot of those in the parish who do not pray, and my heart is sad. So pray that I may take all your sacrifices and prayers to the Lord. Thank you for having responded to my call« (October 4, 1984).

»Dear children. Intend all your evening prayers at home for the conversion of sinners because the world is in great sin. Recite the Rosary every evening« (October 8, 1984 - through Jakov who was ill).

»I call on you to invite everybody to the prayer of the Rosary. By the Rosary you will conquer all the calamities which Satan wants to inflict upon the Catholic Church. Pray the Rosary, all you priests. Devote your time to the Rosary.« This was a message for priests given on the anniversary, June 25, 1985, as an answer to the question of Marija Pavlović: »Our Lady, what would you like to recommend to priests?«

»Dear children: Today I invite you in a particular way to enter the battle against Satan by means of prayer. Satan wants to battle more, now that you are aware of his activity. Dear children, put on, therefore, the armor against Satan, and with the Rosary in your hands you will defeat him. Thank you for your response to my call« (August 8, 1985).

»Dear children: Today I invite you to start praying the Rosary with a living faith. Only in this way shall I be able to help you. You, dear children, want to get favors without praying. In that case I cannot help you because you do not care to move. Dear children, I call on you to pray the Rosary and to accept it as an obligation which you will meet with delight. In doing so you will understand why I have remained so long with you. I want to teach you how to pray. Thank you for having responded to my call« (June 12, 1986).

THE JOYFUL MYSTERIES

JESUS ENTERS INTO MY LIFE

INTRODUCTORY PRAYER: My Lord and my God, I want to devote to you this time of mine. Quiet my heart. Help me to abandon myself completely to you. Do not let any of my words be empty. Let each word be a step closer to you. Enlighten my mind and open my heart so that your Word may grow within it as a seed of love, faith and hope; that it may grow like it did in the immaculate bosom of the Virgin after she, in all humbleness, had accepted to be the handmaid of God. Help me that I also may place myself at your disposal as your faithful servant. I believe in you, Father, in your Son, and in your Holy Spirit. Amen.

(Now first say the Creed and then read or listen to the Biblical words of the prophet Isaiah.)

»Listen, O house of David. Is it not enough for you to weary men, must you also weary my God? Therefore the Lord himself will give you this sign: the virgin shall be with child, and bear a son, and shall name him Emmanuel. He shall be living on curds and honey by the time he learns to reject the bad and the good« (Is 7:13-15).

FIRST JOYFUL MYSTERY: *»In the sixth month, the angel Gabriel was sent from God to a town of Galilee called Nazareth, to a virgin betrothed to a man named Joseph, of the house of David, and the virgin's name was Mary. And coming to her he said, 'Hail, favored one. The Lord is with you.' But she was greatly troubled at what was said and pondered what sort of greeting this might be. Then the angel said to her, 'Do not be afraid, Mary, for you have found favor with God. Behold, you will conceive in your womb and bear a son, and you shall name him Jesus. He will be great and he will be called Son of the Most High, and the Lord God will give him the throne of David his father, and he will rule over the house of Jacob forever, and of his kingdom there will be no end.' But Mary said to the angel, 'How can this be, since I have no relations with a man?' And the angel said to her in reply, 'The holy Spirit will come upon you, and the power of the Most High will overshadow you. Therefore the child to be born will be called holy, the Son of God. And behold, Elizabeth, you relative, has also conceived a son in her old age, and this is the sixth month for her who was called barren; for nothing will be impossible for God.' Mary said, 'Behold, I am the handmaid of the Lord. May it be done to me according to your word'* (Lk 1:26-38).*

Mary, you readily agreed to be the servant of the Lord after having first been troubled and then having thought about the heavenly call. Mary, you are the virgin the prophet Isaiah speaks about. You knew your God so well and walked in his presence. You gave Him your life because you were awaiting the promised Savior. You were not troubled because you were not ready to do His will, but because you could not believe that you were exactly the virgin upon whom the power of the Holy Spirit would come and who would bear Emmanuel, »God with us.« Your fear was not the fear of haughty and selfish men, but the fear of God's humble ones who always readily do God's will, but without self-praise and boasting.

Mary, no wonder you were excited because the night of damnation and the night of salvation and the long awaited dawn bearing the Day, met in you.

Mary, perhaps you had other life plans when God entered into your life with His special plan. And you, as His lowly servant, opened wide the door of your heart to Him. Your example prompts me to turn to the Lord myself and to say to Him: »Come, O Lord. Come. My soul is awaiting you generously and my heart is ready to welcome you. Come into my dreams and into my plans, into my hopes and my fears. Enter into my life and I shall be your servant all my life. I know that I am not worthy to have you under my roof, but I also know that you love sinners and that you constantly search for them. Therefore, O Lord, enter into my darkness, into my hardships and pains. Enter into where you have been expelled by sin. Enter also into those parts of my life where I preferred my own will to your holy will. Enter now while I am meditating and praying before the cross of your Son and before the figure of His Mother who conceived Him by the power of the Holy Spirit.«

(Now recite meditatively one Our Father, ten Hail Marys and at the end, one Glory Be. The following prayer is usually added after each mystery: »O my Jesus, forgive us our sins, save us from the fires of hell, and lead all souls to heaven, especially those who have most need of your mercy.«)

THE SECOND JOYFUL MYSTERY: Mary, you went to visit your cousin Elizabeth. It is God's will that we bring Jesus into the life of other people once He has entered into our life; to bring Him into other people's joys and sorrows, into other people's darkness and bitterness. Therefore, Mary, let my love for the sick grow and become so strong that I may be able to recognize your Son in every sick brother and sister.

(There follows the Our Father, 10 Hail Marys, Glory Be and the invocation O my Jesus...)

THE THIRD JOYFUL MYSTERY: Mary, you are the bearer of the Word and the Mother of salvation. You, who consented to be the servant, become a Mother now. The Lord raises the lowly and that is why you are the Mother of the Savior. You gave birth to the one whom the prophets had announced and for whom the upright had longed. God has entered into my life, too. I also said, »God, I am your servant.« But the fruits of my serving have made me neither a brother nor a sister, neither a father nor a mother to people yet. O Mother of my God, grant that He may completely enter into my life while I am adoring Him.

(Our Father, 10 Hail Marys, Glory Be, O my Jesus...)

THE FOURTH JOYFUL MYSTERY: Mary, I am watching you in my mind as you present your first-born Son to the heavenly Father so that salvation may come through Him. At the presentation you were certainly saying: »O God, here is my Son. He is the fruit of my womb but He belongs to you, as I want to belong to you with all my heart.« I am also standing with you, Mary, in the temple before the Lord and presenting myself to Him following your example. I have received everything, and I give away everything. I do not want to keep anything for myself, either before God or before men.

(Our Father, 10 Hail Marys, Glory Be, O my Jesus...)

THE FIFTH JOYFUL MYSTERY: I watch you, Mary, bringing up your Son with all responsibility. You had taken Him to the temple. The joy of the meeting in the temple turned into a great sorrow for you. For three days you did not know where your Son was and you were unhappy. But your sorrow did not prevent you from doing the Father's will. You went in search of Him and your search was rewarded with a new joy.

Mary, while praying these mysteries I am meditating on how God, after having entered into your life, prepared you for even greater favors. Encouraged by these mysterious events, I say once again, in face of all my trials and fears: »Here I am, O Lord, enter into my life. I want to do your will, even in times of hardships. I want all my crosses and difficulties to bear new meetings with you.«

(Our Father, 10 Hail Marys, Glory Be, O my Jesus...)

CLOSING PRAYER: Thank you, Lord, for my having been able to meditate on your entering into Mary's life and thank you for having prepared her to receive you. You did great things in her life, indeed. I know that you are not going to leave me either, for you have entered into my life. Guide me and give me the grace of letting myself be guided. May it be so. Amen.

THE SORROWFUL MYSTERIES:

JESUS GOES WITH ME THROUGH SUFFERING

Father, your will be done.
In the name of the Father, and...

INTRODUCTORY PRAYER: My Jesus, your coming to this world was wonderful. Wonderful because you were ready to suffer like all men. You were not spared from crosses, yet you were always ready to alleviate other people's pains, to take crosses away, to heal and to comfort. Now a special hour has come. Your personal Calvary is approaching. Death inevitable is approaching. I do not want either to doze or to sleep, but to stay awake with you. Jesus, I wish my prayer could bring you comfort from brothers and sisters who suffer. I wish it could bring you joy and strength from them. Send me your Spirit that I may know how to pray, that I may come closer to you. Amen.

I believe...

THE FIRST SORROWFUL MYSTERY: Jesus, you experienced sorrow and distress in the Garden of Gethsemane. You asked your Father to let the bitter cup pass you by, but you added immediately, »Father, your will be done.« You who had refreshed many a sufferer found yourself in suffering, alone. There was nobody to help you. The Father could have, but you agreed to drink the bitter cup to the last drop. But it must have been an all too bitter agony to make you sweat with blood. I believe that all the agony and all the suffering of the world was present in your bloody sweat. Jesus, thank you for every drop of blood that ran with the sweat. I know that from that moment all the agony of the world became an agony that redeems and an agony that can redeem. I pray to you, for the sake of your sweat, to look upon all those who are seeking the Father's will now. Help also those who have learned the Father's will, but are too weak to accept it. May all their agony be redeemed through a renewed acceptance of the Father's will.

(Remain in silence praying for those who suffer.)

Jesus, open my heart now that I am going to read Luke's account of your agony.

»Then going out he went, as was his custom, to the Mount of Olives, and his disciples followed him. When he arrived at the place he said to them, 'Pray that you may not undergo the test.' After withdrawing about a stone's throw from them and kneeling, he prayed, say-

ing, 'Father, if you are willing, take this cup away from me; still, not my will but yours be done.' And to strengthen him an angel from heaven appeared to him. He was in such agony and he prayed so fervently that his sweat became like drops of blood falling on the ground. When he rose from prayer and returned to his disciples, he found them sleeping from grief. He said to them, 'Why are you sleeping? Get up and pray that you may not undergo the test'« (Lk 22:39-46).

(Our Father, 10 Hail Marys, Glory Be, O my Jesus...)

THE SECOND SORROWFUL MYSTERY: Jesus, you were scourged at Pilate's court. I know what the custom was with scourging. They would tie the condemned person to a post and then the scourgers would deal unmerciful lashes on the body of the condemned person. My Jesus, this act, too, takes my breath away. My heart freezes. However, you magnanimously forgave your scourgers all the blows with which they wounded you all over. Therefore I pray to you to set free with your scourges also those who do not want to do the Father's will and who destroy themselves with scourges which befall them, because they do not decide for forgiveness and love. Thank you for the example of love and forgiveness which manifested itself when they scourged you severely.

(Our Father, 10 Hail Marys, Glory Be, O my Jesus...)

THE THIRD SORROWFUL MYSTERY: My Jesus, they crowned you with the crown of thorns after the scourging. They wrapped you in a scarlet military cloak and made a fool of you - those who were near you, for your friends were far away. When hatred starts forging evil plans, then it is not likely to stop. It was not enough for them to have scourged you so murderously and now they go on mocking you and crowning you with the crown of thorns. But this time, too, hatred and evil were surprised before you. You remained calm in all your suffering. They saw in your behavior that you understood even those who treated you like that. And even more, that you loved them and that you did not condemn them. But their wickedness had no limits. That is what happens when evil has affected a man, a family, a community. Then it never stops destroying. Jesus, look upon all the offended and the humiliated, the scorned and the rejected. Redeem them with your crown of thorns from under the grindstone of torturers and oppressors. Cleanse their heart of every hatred. Do not let them plan revenge and return evil with evil. Jesus, in your name, let forgiveness spread.

(Our Father, 10 Hail Marys, Glory Be, O my Jesus...)

THE FOURTH SORROWFUL MYSTERY: Jesus, you carried your cross to Calvary. All I know about your way of the cross is that it was horrifying. However, in a sea of pain and suffering you had three precious drops of consolation: the meeting with your Mother, Veronica's handkerchief and the brief hand in carrying the cross from Simon the Cyrenean. You certainly appreciated these drops of consolation and rewarded them with consolation and strength. But you may well have wondered at that moment, »Where are the rest whom I have helped so unselfishly?« And I know again you understood them, too, and presented your cross for them as well. Help me, Jesus, to learn something, to be sensitive to other people's pain, to know how to give comfort even in the most difficult moments, that I may never find it hard to shoulder the burden of others. I especially ask you to help us not to aggravate crosses and sufferings for each other. For it is the Father's will for us all to be happy and to love each other even in hard times.

(Our Father, 10 Hail Marys, Glory Be, O my Jesus...)

THE FIFTH SORROWFUL MYSTERY: You commended your spirit to the Father and died on the cross after you had taken the cup given to you by the Father, because you were ready to accept it. I remain speechless here. I shall remain silent before your cross. (In silence, meditate for a while on the events on Calvary.) There is nothing to be said here but only heave a sigh: O, is it possible that human wickedness can go so far? Is the love of God for us so strong that the Father did not even spare his own Son but allowed him to be crucified for our salvation? Is the Father's forgiving love in His Son so great that he pardoned everyone immediately? My Jesus, thank you for having done all this for us. Do teach us to love and to forgive. Strengthen all those who, for the lack of their own love, cannot forgive, and who destroy each other in hatred. Help us all to accept the Father's will as you did, because it is the only way of salvation. We pray to you for the dying. Give them strength to commend their spirits to the

Father in peace. Take them into your peace, O Lord Jesus.

(Our Father, 10 Hail Marys, Glory Be, O my Jesus...)

Meditation: My God, my God, why have you forsaken me, far from my prayer, from the words of my cry? O my God, I cry out by day, and you answer not; by night, and there is no relief for me. Yet you are enthroned in the holy place, O glory of Israel. In you our fathers trusted; they trusted, and you delivered them. To you they cried, and they escaped; in you they trusted, and they were not put to shame (Ps 22(21):2-6).

CLOSING PRAYER

Jesus, may the meditation on your passion and death, on your acceptance of the Father's will and of the cup of suffering from His hand bring me closer to you. May it give me strength for my suffering and bring me closer to those suffering around me. Thank you for what you have done for me. May your passion and death be always in my mind and heart. Amen.

Meditate on Psalms 31(30):12-17 or sing a song of your own choice:

For all my foes I am an object of reproach, a laughingstock to my neighbors, and a dread to my friends; they who see me abroad flee from me. I am forgotten like the unremembered dead; I am like a dish that is broken. I hear the whispers of the crowd, that frighten me from every side, as they consult together against me, plotting to take my life. But my trust is in you, O Lord; I say, 'You are my God.' In your hands is my destiny; rescue me from the clutches of my enemies and my persecutors. Let your face shine upon your servant; save me in your kindness (Ps 31(30):12-17).

Sing or read slowly the following hymn:

> O sacred head surrounded
> By crown of piercing thorn.
> O bleeding head so wounded,
> Reviled and put to scorn.
>
> Our sins have marred the glory
> Of that most holy face.
> Yet angel hosts adore thee,
> And tremble as they gaze.
>
> The Lord of every nation
> Was hung upon a tree;
> His death was our salvation,
> Our sins, his agony.

O Jesus, by thy Passion,
Thy life in us increase;
Thy death for us did fashion
Our pardon and our peace.

THE GLORIOUS MYSTERIES

THE LORD CARRIES ME TO A NEW LIFE

In the name of the Father...
I believe...

INTRODUCTORY PRAYER: I wish to glorify you, O God, for you conquered death in your Son. Open my heart and enlighten my mind that I may be able to glorify you. That is all I am going to ask of you in these mysteries. Enlighten me that I may glorify you. Let my life be for your glory and to the honor of your Son whom you raised from the dead by the power of your Holy Spirit, who livesand reigns in unity with you and theresurrectedSavior. Amen.

THE FIRST GLORIOUS MYSTERY: You rose from the dead gloriously, my Jesus, and so conquered death. Glory be to you, glorious Conqueror. Glory be to you for having opened our tombs and for having brought us out to life. Praise be to you in heaven and on earth. Let all that was doomed to death and destruction glorify you. Let the whole universe praise you. (Jn 14:27)

I am glorifying you with the Church in this canticle:

(Read slowly and in deep contemplation)

Heaven, earth and the universe
Let them exult and sing for joy:
Look, the victory of Jesus
Conquered death and brought us back life.

The time of grace is coming back,
Salvation has dawned upon us.
With the precious blood of the Lamb
The sins of the world have been washed.

On this day of resurrection
A hope's dawning for us mortals:
After death - we all know well -
With Jesus Christ shall we all rise.

Let us sing happy all the time,
Exult in the Resurrected:
The new life will last for ever,
With Christ, Easter has dawned to all.
Amen.

(Our Father, 10 Hail Marys, Glory Be, O my Jesus, forgive us our sins, save us from the fires of hell and lead all souls to heaven, especially those who have most need of your mercy.)

THE SECOND GLORIOUS MYSTERY: I glorify you, O my Jesus, because you did not leave your apostles in suspense but gave them joy with your resurrection and appeared to them for forty days. And then, before their eyes, you went to the Father and were seated at His right hand, for this place was due to you as the conqueror of death. You told the apostles to pray and to wait for help.

We are celebrating with joy
The feast of Jesus' ascension.
Behold, the glorious Lord Christ
Reigns the world at the Father's right.

A bright cloud lifted Him high up
Taking Him from disciples' sight.
But a living and steadfast faith
Can see Him present everywhere.
He was tied with love bonds to us,
Our pains He in His heart does feel:
At Father's right He thinks of us,
And pleads for us before His face.

Let us praise Jesus the Savior
Celebrating His ascension:
With Him we were all lifted up,
Heaven is our eternal home.

(Our Father, 10 Hail Marys, Glory Be, O my Jesus...)

THE THIRD GLORIOUS MYSTERY: We praise you, resurrected Victor, because you sent the Holy Spirit, the Comforter, upon the apostles, who were praying with your Mother, and changed their life. Thank you for having turned their fear into courage, their anxiety into peace, their lack of understanding into the power of testimony to the ends of the world.

> As every year, so does this time
> The day of joy come to us
> When the Spirit, the Comforter,
> Descended on the apostles.
> In the form of the blazing tongues
> The fire of God flickered o'er them,
> Filling their mouths with words of God,
> And heating their hearts to a glow.
>
> As many days after Easter
> Did this event come to pass,
> As many years it once did take
> For Jew, the slave, to be set free.
>
> And now, O God, we pray to you:
> Bestow graciously upon us
> The gifts of your Holy Spirit,
> Which you are sending from above.

(Our Father, 10 Hail Marys, Glory Be, O my Jesus...)

THE FOURTH GLORIOUS MYSTERY: Praise and glory be to you, my Lord, for not having spared your Mother in your suffering. Thank you for the graces you bestowed upon her, enabling her to share in your redemptive act for which reason we are now glorifying her in her assumption. Thank you for having taken her, your humble servant and our Mother, with body and soul, up into heaven. Thank you for opening in her a new way for us, the way of resurrection.

> Like the bright dawn of a new day,
> Like the blazing sun at midday,
> Like the bright moon that shines at night
> Mary was taken up to heaven.
>
> The one whom your bosom once hid,
> The one you laid in a manger,
> You're now watching in Father's glory
> As the King of all Creation.
>
> O woman, blessed above all,
> More than angels and all saints,
> Hear the loud cheers of the whole world
> And of the angels' choirs above.

(Our Father, 10 Hail Marys, Glory Be, O my Jesus...)

THE FIFTH GLORIOUS MYSTERY: Be praised, O my Lord, for having crowned your Mother Mary Queen in heaven. Thank you Mary for having allowed the Lord to be glorified through you.

> You, paramount of all creatures,
> God's Mother, the Queen of heaven.
> Our Creator the most gracious,
> Exalted you above all creation.
>
> Your Son, lifted up on the cross,
> Redeemed the world with His blood,
> You, witness of His agony,
> Became the Mother of us all.
>
> We exult to you today,
> Congratulating your glory
> Look graciously upon us all,
> Keep a watch over your children:
>
> Glory to Father, the All-High,
> With the Son and Holy Spirit,
> For having amply favored you,
> For the diadem on your head.

(Our Father, 10 Hail Marys, Glory Be, O my Jesus...)

CLOSING PRAYER: Thank you, O Lord Jesus Christ, for my having been able, through these glorious mysteries of the Rosary, to feel the power with which you conquered death and sin. Thank you for the joy which you prepared for your Mother by your resurrection, for your apostles, for the whole world, for all creation. Thank you for our not being delivered to death any more, but invited to a new life. Thank you that no one among men, of your brothers and sisters, must end in death and darkness from now on, but rather in light and life. Let my heart sing your praise incessantly from today. Let the song of resurrection, the song of the fullness of life, the song of joy, peace and love never fade from my lips. Let it be so through the intercession of Mary whom you glorified and through whom the Father was glorified in the Holy Spirit who lives and reigns with you, Jesus, and with the Father for ever and ever. Amen.

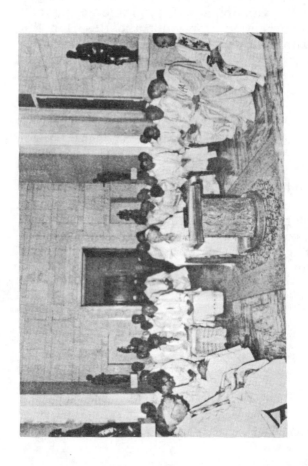

THE ROSARY OF PEACE

Introductory Prayer

Heavenly Father, I believe that you are the good Father of all people. I believe that you sent your Son Jesus Christ to the world to conquer evil and sin, and to accomplish peace among all people, for all people are your children and Jesus' brothers. And once we know this, all destruction and every defilement of peace is all the more pitiable and incomprehensible. Grant now that I and all those who will pray for peace, may pray with a pure heart so that you may answer our prayers and give us true peace of heart and soul - peace to our families, peace to our Church and to the whole world. Good Father, remove from us all weeds of disturbance and disorder and give us the joyous fruits of peace and reconciliation with you and with all men. We ask you this with Mary, the Mother of your Son and the Queen of Peace. May it be so.

I believe...

THE FIRST MYSTERY: Jesus offers peace to my heart.

»Peace I leave with you; my peace I give to you. Not as the world gives do I give it to you.

Do not let your hearts be troubled or afraid«
(Jn 14:27).

Jesus, quiet my heart. Open my heart to your peace. I have had enough unrest and anxiety. Jesus, I have been cheated thoroughly by false hopes, bruised by heavy blows, cut by sharp blades. I have no peace. I am easily overwhelmed by worries. I am easily affected by fear and mistrust. Too often have I hoped to find peace in this world, but my heart is still restless. Therefore, Jesus, together with St. Augustine I ask you to appease my heart and let it find rest in you. Do not ever let the waves of sin overflow it. Be my rock and my fortress from now on. Come back to me and stay with me, you who are the only fountain of my true peace. Thank you for the consoling words recorded by your dearest disciple:

»I have told you this so that you might have peace in me. In the world you will have trouble, but take courage, I have conquered the world«
(Jn 16:33).

(Our Father, 10 Hail Marys, Glory Be, O my Jesus...)

THE SECOND MYSTERY: Jesus offers peace to my family.

»Whatever town or village you enter, look for a worthy person in it, and stay there until

you leave. As you enter a house, wish it peace. If the house is worthy, let you peace come upon it; if not, let your peace return to you« (Mt 10:11-13).

O Jesus, thank you for having thought of our families as well. Thank you for having sent out the apostles to spread their peace in families. Now I ask you heartily to make my family deserving of your peace. Cleanse us of all sinful thoughts and deeds that your peace may grow and come into bloom within us. May your peace remove all anxieties, all conflicts from our family. Grant that your peace may completely overwhelm us and that you, the Peacemaker, may always be the first member of our family. I also pray to you for neighboring families. Let them, too, be filled with your peace and we shall all be fine.

(Our Father, 10 Hail Marys, Glory Be, O my Jesus...)

THE THIRD MYSTERY: Jesus offers peace to the Church and calls her to spread peace.

»If anyone is in Christ, he is a new creation. The old order has passed away; now all is new. All this has been done by God who has reconciled us to himself through Christ and has given us the ministry of reconciliation. We implore

you in Christ's name: be reconciled to God« (2 Cor 5:17-19).

Jesus, I implore you to give peace to your Church. Reconcile all that is still unreconciled in her. Bless priests, bishops and the Pope that they may live reconciled and perform the ministry of reconciliation. Remove from your Church all unreconciliation. Reconcile all those who are at variance in your Church and who, with their mutual conflicts, scandalize your little ones. Reconcile various religious groups. May your Church, spotless and stainless, be steadily calm, and let her be the promoter of peace.

(Our Father, 10 Hail Marys, Glory Be, O my Jesus...)

THE FOURTH MYSTERY: Jesus offers peace to His people.

»As he drew near, he saw the city and wept over it, saying, 'If this day you only knew what makes for peace - but now it is hidden from your eyes. For the days are coming upon you when your enemies will raise a palisade against you; and they will encircle you and hem you in on all sides. They will smash you to the ground and your children within you, and they will not leave one stone upon another within you because you did not recognize the time of your visitation'« (Lk 19:41-44).

Jesus, you wept over your city and over your people. You offered them peace, but they were deaf and blind and did not either hear or see. Thank you for your love toward your people. Please grant that I may know how to lead my people, my town, my village, and my homeland to the good. I pray to you for every individual member of my homeland, for each of my countrymen, for all those who are in authority. Grant that they may not be blind but that they may learn and recognize what they are to do for the realization of peace. Let there be no more ruin in my people, but let them all become solid spiritual buildings which will shine with peace and joy. Jesus, give peace to my people. Give peace to every nation. Let everyone live in peace and let everyone proclaim peace.

(Our Father, 10 Hail Marys, Glory Be, O my Jesus...)

THE FIFTH MYSTERY: Jesus offers peace to the whole world.

»Promote the welfare of the city to which I have exiled you; pray for it to the Lord, for upon its welfare depends your own« (Jer 29:7).

Jesus, the dangerous seed of wars and all kinds of conflicts have long since been sown and are now germinating on the earth. And I know quite well that my peace too, as well as the peace of all people, firmly depends on peace in all countries and nations of the world. Therefore I ask you to root out, with your divine power, the ill-fated seed of unrest and sin as the first cause of every disturbance. Let the whole world be open to your peace. All people need you in their life's unrest, so help them all to find peace, to realize peace. Many nations have lost their character. Many live in fear of others who are stronger and richer. Many of the poor and the persecuted rebel, while many of the rich and the wanton vent their fury over them. Generally, there is no peace, or hardly any. So, Lord, send us your Holy Spirit that He may bring the original divine order into this human disorder of ours. Let the nations be healed of their spiritual wounds so that mutual reconciliation may be possible. Send to all nations the messengers and harbingers of peace so that everyone may realize the deep truth of what you once said through your great prophet: »How beautiful upon the mountains are the feet of Him who brings glad tidings, announcing peace, bearing good news, announcing salvation, and saying to Zion, 'Your God is King'« (Is 52:7).

(Our Father, 10 Hail Marys, Glory Be, O my Jesus...)

CLOSING PRAYER

O Lord, heavenly Father, give us your peace. We ask this of you together with all your children in whom you have planted the desire for peace and appeasement. We ask this together with all those who, in unspeakable sufferings, are sighing for peace. And after this life, which, for the best part of it after all, we have spent in restlessness, take us into the Kingdom of your eternal peace and love. Accept also all those who have fallen as victims of wars and conflicts. Accept also those who are looking for peace on wrong paths. We ask this through Christ, the Prince of Peace, and through the intercession of our heavenly Mother, the Queen of Peace. Amen.

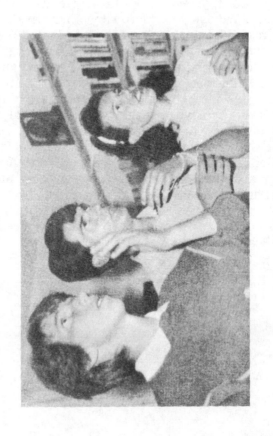

THE JESUS ROSARY

In the name of the Father...

INTRODUCTORY PRAYER

Jesus, my Savior, I want to be together with you now. You are my brother and my Savior. You have remained with me and because of me. Thank you. Grateful for your life, Jesus, I give up my life to you now, at the beginning of this prayer. I leave all worries, all problems, all that attracts me and so draws me away from you. I renounce sin by which I used to destroy our friendship, I renounce evil by which I used to jeopardize our communion. I lay aside at your feet all I have, Jesus, and want to be totally yours and - together with you the Father's.

Mary, no one knew how to be with Jesus as well as you did, for he grew up and developed at your side. Be with me now that I may know and be able to be with Jesus. Mary, pray with me that the Spirit of Jesus may descend upon me, that he may pray in me and say again: »Abba, Father.« Amen.

I believe...

THE FIRST MYSTERY: Jesus was born in Bethlehem.

»And Joseph to went up from Galilee from the town of Nazareth to Judea, to the city of David that is called Bethlehem, because he was of the house and the family of David, to be enrolled with Mary, his betrothed, who was with child. While they were there, the time came for her to have her child, and she gave birth to her first-born son. She wrapped him in swaddling clothes and laid him in a manger because there was no room for them in the inn« (Lk 2:4-7).

»The angel said to them, 'Do not be afraid; for behold, I proclaim to you good news of great joy that will be for all the people. For today in the city of David a savior has been born for you who is the Messiah and Lord. And this will be a sign for you: you will find an infant wrapped in swaddling clothes and lying in a manger.' And suddenly there was a multitude of the heavenly host with the angel, praising God and saying: 'Glory to God in the highest and on earth peace to those on whom his favor rests'« (Lk 2:10-14).

Intention: Let us pray for peace. (In these or in your own words.) Jesus, be peace to us all. Remove the obstacles which divide us from each other. Make us the people of good will.

5 Our Fathers   (Pray deeply and slowly)

»O Jesus, be our protection and strength.«

THE SECOND MYSTERY: Jesus helps and gives everything for the poor.

»As sunset approached, the twelve came and said to him: 'Dismiss the crowd so that they can go into the villages and farms in the neighborhood and find themselves lodging and food, for this is certainly an out of the way place.' He answered them, 'Why do you not give them something to eat yourselves?' They replied, 'We have nothing but five loaves and two fish...' Then taking the five loaves and two fish, Jesus raised His eyes to heaven, pronounced a blessing over them, broke them, and gave them to his disciples for distribution to the crowd. They all ate until they had enough. What they had left, over and above, filled twelve baskets« (Lk 9:12-13; 16-17).

Intention: Let us pray for the Holy Father, and for all responsible persons in the world.

Jesus, you loved the poor and gave them earthly bread. But moreover, you offer heavenly bread to all who are hungry and thirsty. Move the heart of our Pope and all responsible persons in the Church and in all countries that they may help distribute the goods of the earth justly so that all may eat their fill and leave some over and above.

5 Our Fathers

»O Jesus, be our protection and strength.«

THE THIRD MYSTERY: Jesus surrenders completely to the Father and does His will.

»Then Jesus came with them to a place called Gethsemane, and he said to his disciples, 'Sit here while I go over there and pray.' He took along Peter and the two sons of Zebedee, and he began to feel sorrow and distress. He said to them, 'My soul is sorrowful even unto death. Remain here and keep watch with me.' He advanced a little and fell prostrate in prayer, saying, 'My Father, if it is possible, let this cup pass from me; yet, not as I will, but as you will'« (Mt 26:36-39).

»Withdrawing a second time, he prayed again, 'My Father, if it is not possible that this cup pass without my drinking it, your will be done.' Then he returned once more and found them asleep, for they could not keep their eyes open. He left them and withdrew again and prayed a third time, saying the same thing again« (Mt 26:42-44).

Intention: We pray for priests and for all those who are called to serve Jesus in a special way all their life.

Jesus, as you surrendered to the Father's will even in the most difficult moments, grant grace to all priests and to all consecrated persons that they may persevere in doing the Father's will. Disperse their fear of the cup of their life. Let them turn all bitterness and loneliness of life into the way of resurrection.

5 Our Fathers

»O Jesus, be our protection and strength.«

THE FOURTH MYSTERY: Jesus knew He was going to give His life for us and did so freely, for He loves us.

»When Jesus had said this, he raised his eyes to heaven and said, 'Father, the hour has come. Give glory to your son, so that your son may glorify you, just as you gave him authority over all people, so that he may give eternal life to all you gave him'« (Jn 17:1-2).

»And I consecrate myself for them, so that they also may be consecrated in truth« (Jn 17:19).

Intention: Let us pray for families.

Jesus, you loved us, that is why you went away to the Father so calm and resigned. Nothing was too difficult, for you were borne away by love for us. Fill our families with readiness to do everything for each other so that they may be happy. Let all fathers and mothers consecrate their life to love so that they may be able to consecrate themselves to their sons and daughters.

5 Our Fathers

»O Jesus, be our protection and strength.«

THE FIFTH MYSTERY: Jesus made His life a sacrifice for us.

»This is my commandment: love one another as I love you. No one has greater love than this, to lay down one's life for one's friends. You are my friends if you do what I command you« (Jn 15:12-14).

Intention: Let us pray that each of us may be willing to lay down his life for his neighbor.

Jesus, you showed the greatest love by giving your life for our salvation. You left all the glory you had from the beginning and took on the form of a servant. You invited us to do the same, to be ready to live with and for each other, up to the end, as you did for us. Thank you for enabling us to love. Destroy selfishness, haughtiness, hatred, jealousy, and narrow mindedness in us.

5 Our Fathers

»O Jesus, be our protection and strength.«

THE SIXTH MYSTERY: Jesus conquered Satan by His resurrection.

»While they were puzzling over this, behold, two men in dazzling garments appeared to them. They were terrified and bowed their

faces to the ground. They said to them, 'Why do you seek the living one among the dead? He is not here, but he has been raised. Remember what he said to you while he was still in Galilee, that the Son of Man must be handed over to sinners and be crucified, and rise on the third day'« (Lk 24:4-7).

»The seventy-two returned rejoicing, and said, 'Lord, even the demons are subject to us because of your name.' Jesus said, 'I have observed Satan fall like lightning from the sky. Behold, I have given you the power to tread upon serpents and scorpions and upon the full force of the enemy and nothing will harm you. Nevertheless, do not rejoice because the spirits are subject to you, but rejoice because your names are written in heaven'« (Lk 10:17-20).

Intention: Let us pray that sin may disappear, that Jesus may resurrect in us.

Jesus, conqueror of death, conquer sin and death in me. Conquer hatred in me and in others, that peace may come. By the power of your word and by the power of a priest's word drive away the influence of Satan.

5 Our Fathers

»O Jesus, be our protection and strength.«

THE SEVENTH MYSTERY: Jesus ascends into heaven.

»Then he led them [out] as far as Bethany, raised his hands, and blessed them. As he blessed them he parted from them and was taken up to heaven. They did him homage and then returned to Jerusalem with great joy, and were continually in the temple praising God« (Lk 24:50-53).

Intention: Let us pray that the will of God may be done and fulfilled.

Jesus, give us the spirit of prayer and joy that we may testify to you with our life in every tribe and nation. Let your Church be a permanent witness to your immense love in the world.

- 3 Our Fathers

»O Jesus, be our protection and strength.«

THE EIGHTH MYSTERY: Jesus sends His Holy Spirit upon the apostles and His Mother Mary.

»When the time for Pentecost was fulfilled, they were all in one place together. And suddenly there came from the sky a noise like a strong driving wind, and it filled the entire house in which they were. Then there appeared to them tongues as of fire, which parted and came to rest on each one of them. And they were all filled with the Holy Spirit and began to speak in different tongues, as the Spirit enabled them to proclaim« (Acts 2:1-4).

Intention: Let us pray for the outpouring of the Holy Spirit in his fullness on our families, on the whole Church, on all the religious communities, on all the baptized, on all people, especially on those who decide on the fate of the world, that the Holy Spirit might inspire in them good thoughts and good decisions and may he guide their steps towards peace.

Jesus, send us your Holy Spirit as you sent him upon your apostles and your Mother Mary. May he continually inspire us, may he guide us, and introduce us into his truth. May he teach us love, and may he guide our steps towards peace.

7 Glory Bes

»O Jesus, be our protection and strength.«

CLOSING PRAYER

Jesus, it is good to be with you. Thank you. Thank you for your life, for your love of the Father and for your surrender to the will of the Father. Thank you for having opened the way of salvation to us. Mary, help us to remain faithful on the way of salvation and to come into our eternal glory. Amen.

PRAYER BEFORE CONFESSION

In the name of the Father, and of the Son, and of the Holy Spirit. Amen.

1. Almighty, merciful and good Father, here I am before you on my knees. I want to confess my sins and offenses to you. Father, I am coming back to you like that prodigal son. I confess that I have sinned and that I no longer deserve to be called your son. Kneeling before you, I beg you to throw your arms around my neck just as the good father hugged his son who had squandered his money and ruined himself, and only then remembered his father's love. Father, look on me as you looked through the eyes of your Son, Jesus Christ, when the woman sinner stood before Him, and He did not condemn her. Grant me the grace of contrition and of deep concentration that I may be able to stand in your presence and to start a new life in the light of your Word.

Father, by the power of your Spirit, take the hard, stony heart out of my chest and give me, through this confession, a renewed heart, washed with your love, healed with your mercy. Cleanse my heart and soul that I may receive the ring on my finger as a sign of a renewed and strengthened bond. Give me the robe of peace and love and admit me again to your table. Through sin I have broken off friendship with you.

Father, thank you for your Son's having spoken to us about your mercy in such wonderful parables as:

»*While he was still a long way off, his father caught sight of him, and was filled with compassion. He ran to his son, embraced him and kissed him. The son said to him, 'Father, I have sinned against heaven and against you; I no longer deserve to be called your son.' But his father ordered his servants, 'Quickly bring the finest robe and put it on him; put a ring on his finger and sandals on his feet. Take the fattened calf and slaughter it. Then let us celebrate with a feast, because this son of mine was dead, and has come to life again; he was lost, and has been found'*« (Lk 15:20-24).

Father, grant me grace that I may feel joy already now, while preparing to meet you in confession. Let every fear and hesitation disappear that I may know how to confess my sins. Send me your Spirit that I may remember my sins. Give me the strength to open my soul before you in simplicity and sincerity and not to keep any of my sins secret.

2. Mary, Mother of peace and reconciliation, you called us, as your children, to peace and reconciliation with the Father.

Thank you that many here in Međugorje and in the world have heard your call and have come to be reconciled in a contrite, holy confession. Thank you that many have found peace and inner freedom because they responded to your call when you appeared with a cross and said through tears: »Be reconciled.«

O Mary, grant that, with your help, I may understand the horror of sin. Obtain by prayer the grace for me to weep over my sins and faults with which I have stirred up unrest and hatred, defiled the Father's name, obstructed the coming of His reign, and destroyed joy, love and hope in others around me. Mother Mary, help me understand the depth of your Son's suffering which you witnessed. Grant that my heart may decide for the struggle against sin and sinful habits. My Immaculate Mother, help me to return to the Father's house of togetherness and peace. Awaken within me the awareness of my responsibility for my own self and for others around me, and especially for the plans the Father reveals through you.

I am sorry that your words refer to me, too:

»Dear children: ...You are still ready to commit sin and give yourselves up into

the hands of Satan without thinking...«
(May 25, 1987)

I still sin and find excuses for my sin. I often blame others and think that they are responsible for what I do. Whenever I find an excuse for my evil deeds and my evil words, I know that I consciously collaborate with Satan who wants to keep me in sin, far from the kingdom of peace and love. Mary, obtain by prayer the power of the Holy Spirit that I may now, in silence, feel my sin and confess it.

3. Ask yourself in silence:

What are my sins? Hatred of others, unwillingness to be reconciled to someone, engaging in fortunetelling and sorcery, cursing, damning, blaspheming and dirty language in general, negligence of prayer, neglect of Holy Mass, absent-mindedness in prayer and at Mass, disrespect for elders and superiors, drunkenness, killing, drugs...

Parents, especially, should ask themselves here whether they have killed unborn children by any form of abortion and whether they have confessed this sin. Let spouses ask themselves whether they have cheated on each other and whether they have really born as many children as they could have, and whether they have lived their parenthood responsibly.

For the young especially: Do I endeavor to work, learn and study hard? If not, then I indulge in laziness and do not develop according to God's plan. I remain open to every evil, and so shall not be able, as a completely developed person to contribute to the welfare of my family, community or society. And this is the most dangerous sin for us young, if we consciously or unconsciously resist the development of the gifts God has given us. This bears consequences for the entire life. Do I respect my parents and elders enough? Do I disturb the basic order in the family? Do I embitter the life of my parents and neighbors, instead of trying to make them happy?

Have I been spending too much time in front of a television set, watching films presenting an immoral lifestyle, especially deliberately watching films which present sexuality and relations among people in an unbecoming manner? Have I played with my own body in a degrading manner, bringing myself to sexual pleasure, especially inducing or seducing others into it? If I do this, I bring disorder into my life, which has bitter consequences for my future and the future of others. God has created me as a sexual being, but I have been called to grow in respect of my own self and of others that one day I could live my life the way God wants me to. If, in the evening, I read or watch worthless programs on television, then I disturb the normal night's rest and open a way to mental illnesses. If I do so, I behave irresponsibly to myself, destroy myself and check my personal growth. This is exactly the secret of sin: it destroys me and does not allow me to grow positively.

I also ask myself: Have I been affected by haughtiness, greed, selfishness, laziness, or have I perhaps started to run excessively after material goods, neglecting spiritual ones?

(Remain in silence and examine of your conscience until you have become quite aware of your sins and offenses, of their danger to your life and to the life of others. Then pray.)

Heavenly Father, good and merciful, holy and worthy of my respect, you know my heart and my evil habits. In the light of your love I see how I have misused your goodness. Today I repent with my whole heart. I am sorry. Please, forgive me.

4. Mother Mary, you have come in the name of the Father and want to make me open to the Father's plans. You call me not only to leave sin, every evil and cooperation with evil, but also to teach me to cooperate positively with the Father's will. You want to encourage me by constantly assuring me that I am important for the plan of salvation. Therefore, you have called me, in the Father's name, to grow in love every day and to bring peace to others. Oh Lady, inspire my enthusiasm for cooperation in the plan of building my life and the life of the whole world, and it will be even clearer to me what sin means. Help me to understand that it is not enough to keep a gift but that it must be developed. Help me discover the possibilities of cooperation with the Father's will, and through your intercession, remove all the obstacles in my way. Help me to understand that I am responsible for the good I have missed in myself and in others.

Therefore, I not only ask myself whether I have blasphemed and defamed God's name, but also whether I have always endeavored to glorify His name. Have I really prayed with the heart, finding time for prayer that it may be a true communion. I also seriously ask myself how I have prayed.

Have I really taken every opportunity to love God above all and every man as myself?

Have I tried to use every opportunity to do something for peace, or have I thrown obstacles in the way of peace? When I was aware of problems in this or that family, did I remain inactive instead of helping with my prayers and fasting to bring peace to that family?

Have I resisted God's will consciously and thus remained half-hearted?

Have I helped others by my good example and words?

Have I given freely of my material goods? Or, have I spent money on unnecessary things such as cigarettes, make-up, newspapers or alcohol, while I could have given it to the disposal of others for their daily bread?

Have I tried with all my heart to make good for the injustice I have done to others by hatred, jealousy or envy?

O my God, merciful Father, thank you for helping me to understand that sin is not only an evil that I do, but that it is also what I have failed to do or could have done better. I promise to do everything to conquer sin and all evil habits in myself, and to develop all that is good and positive in me and in others. Help me, Father.

Mary, be with me now and remain with me always so that my decisions may be real and firm.

5. Father, through your Son Jesus Christ, grant, I pray to you, that all who confess here in Medugorje and in the whole world may come to know their sin, repent, make firm decisions and choose the way of conversion and renewal of life. Jesus, destroy evil through every confession: my personal evil, the evil in our families, in the Church and in the whole world. Let the grace of reconciliation spread and bring spiritual and physical health and healing to everybody. Let every confession ward off all trials and Satan's traps from everybody. Let everybody come out of their unconscious collaboration with evil and come into full cooperation with you.

6. Jesus, you sent your apostles to go out into the world and to forgive sins in your name. Thank you for having given such power to men. Therefore, I consciously pray to you for all confessors in the world, especially I pray to you for the priest who is going to hear my confession now and who will give me absolution from my sins and bring rec-

onciliation with you. I pray to you for N. (Mention the priest's name.) Inspire him with your Spirit that he may know how to console and encourage me, that he may know how to lead me on the way of spiritual growth and warn me of the obstacles I place in my path. Bestow on him the grace of love that he, too, may accept me in spite of my sinfulness. Grant that he may always be ready to dispense the grace of reconciliation.

7. Mary, protect all confessors and help them. You are the Mother of all priests, because you are the Mother of the First High Priest. Father, I ask all this in the name of Jesus Christ, your Son in the Holy Spirit, with Mary, your lowly servant. Amen.

Closing Prayer

We adore you, O Christ, and we bless you, because by your Holy Cross, you have redeemed the world.

»Therefore, let us be on our guard while the promise of entering into his rest remains, that none of you seem to have failed. For in fact we have received the good news just as they did. But the word they heard did not profit them, for they were not united in faith with those who listened« (Heb 4:1-2).

»In their affliction, they shall look for me: 'Come, let us return to the Lord, for it is he who has rent, but he will heal us; he has struck us, but he will bind our wounds. He will revive us after two days; on the third day he will raise us up, to live in his presence'« (Hos 6:1-2).

Father, over the tomb of your Son, I am meditating on the word you said to me through the prophet and the apostle. Here I am. Heal me. Raise me up that, with all creatures, I may give glory to your new creation, the creation you started on the third day after the death of your Son. Create me anew so that I may serve you completely and one day exult in you forever.

Mary, with you I want to live everyday in the hope that the promises given to our fathers through the prophets will be fulfilled in me as well. May it be so, and let it be fulfilled in me and in all people. Amen.

PRAYER ON FAST DAYS

Our Lady's call:

»I would like the world to pray with me these days. As much as possible, to fast strictly on Wednesdays and Fridays, to pray every day at least the Rosary; the Joyful, Sorrowful and Glorious mysteries...« (August 14, 1984)

O Lord God, Creator of all creation and my Creator, today we give you thanks for having arranged the world so wonderfully. Thank you for having given fertility to mother earth so that she may bear all kinds of fruit. Thank you for the food prepared from the fruits of the earth. Father, I rejoice in your creatures. I rejoice in all the fruits today, and I thank you. Thank you for our daily food and drink.

Father, thank you for having made my body in such a way as to be able to use the fruits of the earth and so develop and serve you. Thank you, Father, for all those who, through their work, produce new life possibilities. Thank you for those who have much and give away to others. Thank you for all who are hungry for heavenly bread while eating this earthly bread.

Father, thank you also for those who have nothing to eat today, for I am convinced that you will send them help through good people. Father, today I decide to fast. In doing so I do not despise your creatures. I do not renounce them, I only want to rediscover their value. I decide for fasting because your prophets used to fast, because Jesus Christ fasted and so did his apostles and disciples. I especially decide for fasting because your servant, Mother Mary fasted, too. She called me to fasting:

»**Dear children: Today I invite you to start fasting with the heart. There are a lot of people who fast because others do so. Fasting is a habit nobody wants to give up. I ask the parish to fast out of gratitude that God allowed me to stay in this parish so long. Dear children, fast and pray with the heart. Thank you for having responded to my call**« (September 20, 1984).

Father, I present this day of fasting to you. Through fasting I want to listen to and live your word more. I want, during this day, to learn to be turned more toward you, in spite of all the things that surround me. With this fast that I take upon myself freely, I pray to you for all who are hungry and who, because of their hunger, have become aggressive.

I present you this fast for PEACE in the world. Wars come because we are attached to material things and are ready to kill each other because of them.

Father, I present to you this fast for all those who are totally tied down to material things so that they are unable to see any other values. I ask you for all those who are in conflict because they have become blind in what they possess. Father, open our eyes through fasting to what you give us, to what we have. I am also sorry for the blindness which has taken hold of my senses so that I do not give thanks for the goods I have. I repent every misuse of material goods because I used to judge their value wrongly.

Make me able, through this fast today, to see you and the people around me better. Enable me to hear your word better. Through today's fasting, let love for you and for my neighbor grow in me. Father, I decide to live on bread and water today that I may better understand the value of heavenly bread, and the presence of your Son in the Eucharist. Let my faith and trust grow through fasting. Father, I decide for fasting and accept it because I know that in this way my longing for you will grow in me. Eagerly and with gratitude do I think of your Son's words: »How blessed are the poor in spirit: the reign of God is theirs.«

Father, make me poor before you. Grant me grace that through fasting I may understand how much I need you. Grant that through fasting my desire for you may grow, that my heart may long for you as the deer longs for the running waters and the desert for the clouds of rain. Father, I pray to you, grant that through this fast my understanding of the hungry and the thirsty, of those who do not have enough of material goods, may especially grow. Help me see what I do not need but possess, that I may give it up for the benefit of my brothers and sisters.

O Father, I especially pray to you. Grant me the grace to become aware that I am but a pilgrim on this earth, that, when passing away to the other world I shall not take anything with me but love and good deeds. Let the awareness grow within me that even when I possess something I cannot call it my own for I have only received it from you to manage it. Father, grant me grace that through fasting I may become humbler and more willing to do your will.

Cleanse me of my selfishness and haughtiness. Through this fast cleanse me of all bad habits and calm down my passions, and let virtue increase in me. Let the depth of my soul open to your grace through this fast so that it may totally affect and cleanse me. Help me to be always like your Son in trials and temptations; to resist every temptation, so as to be able to serve you and seek your Word more and more, day after day.

Mary, you were free in your heart and bound to nothing except the Father's will. Obtain by prayer the grace of a joyful fast for me today, in which my heart will be able to sing with you a thanksgiving song. Obtain by prayer the grace for me that my decision to fast may be firm and lasting. And I offer, for all people, the difficulties and the hunger I am going to feel today. Mary, pray for me. Let every evil and temptation of Satan stay away from me today through your intercession and through the power of your protection. Teach me, Mary, to fast and to pray that day after day I may become more and more like you and your Son, Jesus Christ, in the Holy Spirit. Amen.

ADORATION OF CHRIST IN THE MOST BLESSED SACRAMENT

1. Holy, holy, holy, Jesus in the Most Blessed Sacrament. Yes, holy and all holy are you, Jesus. You are silently present in a simple small piece of bread. You are in front of me. Grant that I may understand with the heart that you are alive here for me and because of me. Fill me with living faith that you are here and that I am before you. O Jesus, grant me grace that I may adore you with all my being; soul, spirit and body.

O all you saints and angels, be here now. Adore the living Lord Jesus Christ with me. Mary, Mother of my Savior and Mother of us all, be with us too. You called me to adore Jesus and assured me that I would not be alone at this moment before your living Son. Thank you for this message:

»**This evening, too, dear children, I am grateful in a special way that you are here. Adore the Most Blessed Sacrament all the time. I am always present when the faithful are adoring. Special graces are received then**« (March 15, 1984).

O Mary, thank you for your presence.

Like St. Thomas I would like to say this evening: »My Lord and my God.« I am not asking you, Lord Jesus, to hold out your hands with wounds in them for me. I believe that you are alive here and that you are really present with the fullness of your life and love. I remain in silence before you.

(Keep silent and meditate.)

Our Father, Hail Mary, Glory Be

(Then sing this or some other Eucharistic song.)

Holy, holy, holy; holy and all holy, Jesus in the Most Blessed Sacrament.

Meditation: »And men shall say, 'Truly there is a reward for the just; truly there is a God who is judge on earth'« (Ps 58:12).

2. Jesus, you are my God. You are the fountain of holiness and holiness itself. Only to you is my adoration due, to nobody else. Therefore I leave all things, all persons, and all programs. I leave everything to adore you. I want my heart and my mind to become one with you. I give myself up to you with all my being.

Mother Mary, I realize how unworthy I am to adore Jesus. Thank you for being with me. You are worthy of adoring and loving Him more than anybody else in the world, because you are His Mother, loving and faithful. So, Mary, to you do I give my heart that you may adore Jesus in me and with me. To you do I commit my family, my friends, my community, my people and my Church.

O my Mother, I love you immensely and offer myself to you. Through your goodness, love and grace, save me. I want to be yours. I love you endlessly and I want you to protect me. I ask you, Mother of goodness, with my whole heart, to give me your goodness that I may be able to love everybody as you loved Jesus Christ. And I also ask the grace that I may be gracious to you. I present myself completely to you and want you to be with me at every step, for you are full of grace. Amen.

(Eucharistic song or meditate on the following Psalms:

»Bless the Lord, O my soul. O Lord, my God, you are great indeed. You are clothed with majesty and glory, robed in light as with a cloak. You have spread out the heavens like a tent cloth« (Ps 104(103):1-2).

»I will sing to the Lord all my life; I will sing praise to my God while I live. Pleasing to him be my theme; I will be glad in the Lord« (Ps 104(103):33-34).

3. Jesus, you loved me unto death and beyond it. You were born for me, you lived

for me, you died and rose for me. When you realized that death would separate you from me, your love was inventive. You remained with me and for me in the Most Blessed Sacrament. O be praised, Jesus, in this simple bread, in this host. Be praised, you who are all worthy of all praise and glory.

Praise and glory to the Father who sent you to give yourself to us and for us in this way. Praise and glory to the Holy Spirit who, through Mary's intercession, is crying for joy through me. Praise and glory forever and ever.

Therefore, I adore you in every church in the world. Be praised and glorified in every host.

Be praised and glorified in every Communion in which I have met you. Be praised and glorified for all those meetings when I received you without being fully aware that you, the living and true God, had come to me. Be praised and glorified for every moment which I have passed with you so far and which I am going to pass with you in the future. Be praised and glorified in all those who live in love, because they have received you and are inspired by your love. Be praised also in all those who forget you, who do not adore you. Be praised also in all who oppose or persecute you. Be praised and glorified in all who receive you but do not think of your presence, nor live in it, but come back from Holy Communion or Mass as if they had not met you at all. O, be praised and glorified because you are alive now and want to present everyone around you with love and fullness of life.

(Remain in silence and let these words echo in you.)

Our Father, Hail Mary, Glory Be

(In case of a communal adoration, sing an Eucharistic song or meditate on the following Psalms:

»Alleluia! Praise the Lord, O my soul; I will praise the Lord all my life; I will sing praise to my God while I live« (Ps 146(145):1-2).

»Who keeps faith forever, secures justice for the oppressed, gives food to the hungry. The Lord sets captives free; the Lord gives sight to the blind. The Lord raises up those that were bowed down; the Lord loves the just. The Lord protects strangers; the fatherless and the widow he sustains, but the way of the wicked he thwarts. The Lord shall reign forever; your God, O Zion, through all generations. Alleluia« (Ps 146(145):7-10).

4. Lord Jesus, let every word I say during this hour of adoration be in your Spirit. Do not let my words be empty. Inspire me to

understand your Word which you pronounced to draw me completely to you. You
said you were bread for our soul, for our
life, for every hunger, but first and foremost
for the hunger of love. Jesus, feed my soul,
for I am adoring you.

*»So they said to him, "What sign can you do,
that we may see and believe in you? What can
you do? Our ancestors ate manna in the desert,
as it is written: 'He gave them bread from
heaven to eat'"«* (Jn 6:30).

*»So Jesus said to them, 'Amen, amen, I say
to you, it was not Moses who gave the bread
from heaven; my Father gives you true bread
from heaven. For the bread of God is that
which comes down from heaven and gives life
to the world.'*

*So they said to him, 'Sir, give us this bread
always.'*

*Jesus said to them, 'I am the bread of life;
whoever comes to me will never hunger, and
whoever believes in me will never thirst'«* (Jn
6:32-35).

Attracted by your word which applies to
me as well, I am here, Jesus, beseeching you
to give me to eat, and give me to drink. I am
hungry and thirsty. Nothing else can appease my hunger or my thirst, for everything
is transient, everything is deficient. Thank

you for being an answer to my hunger and thirst.

(Remain in silence)

Jesus, here I am kneeling in the name of all those who are hungering and thirsting for truth, justice, love, and reconciliation. I am kneeling in the name of all the children who are hungry for the motherly bread of love and of their parents' home. I am kneeling in the name of all the thirsty who, on the road of this life, are seeking those drinks which make them drunk and lead to death, not to life. O bread of eternal life, I am kneeling before you in the name of all who are quarreling and waging wars, who hate or persecute each other, who behave jealously toward each other because of earthly bread. Jesus, reveal yourself to them as the eternal, heavenly bread. Let them find you and feel your presence so that they will wander no more about the world, beaten up with evil and sin. Jesus, the manna of the Father for us travelers and pilgrims through the desert of this world, I also pray to you for all those who are hungry for earthly bread, who work, but do not get paid, because the stronger and the richer exploit them.

Jesus, I am kneeling before you. Let my heart plunge into your presence and let your life completely absorb me so that, from now on, I may be a sweetness to all who are seeking you, that I may never again embitter life for anybody. Let me become the bread of life with you.

(Silence)

Our Father, Hail Mary, Glory Be

(A Eucharistic song or meditation on the following Psalms:

»But the kindness of the Lord is from eternity to eternity toward those who fear him, and his justice toward children's children among those who keep his covenant and remember to fulfill his precepts. The Lord has established his throne in heaven, and his kingdom rules over all. Bless the Lord, all you his angels, you mighty in strength, who do his bidding, obeying his spoken word. Bless the Lord, all you his hosts, his ministers, who do his will. Bless the Lord, all his works, everywhere in his domain. Bless the Lord, O my soul« (Ps 103(102):17-22).

5. Jesus, the bread of life, the life of the world, incomprehensible secret, the Father's Word to us all, I am at peace with you. Now, I am meditating on another word of yours which on one occasion was recommended by your Mother:

»No man can serve two masters. He will either hate one and love the other or be attentive to one and despise the other. You cannot

give yourselves to God and money. I warn you then: do not worry about your livelihood, what you are to eat or drink or use for clothing. Is not life more than food? Is not the body more valuable than clothes? Look at the birds in the sky. They do not sow or reap, they gather nothing into barns; yet your heavenly Father feeds them. Are not you more important than they? Which of you by worrying can add a moment to his life span?

As for clothes, why be concerned? Learn a lesson from the way the wild flowers grow. They do not work; they do not spin. Yet I assure you, not even Solomon in all his splendor was arrayed like one of these. If God can clothe in such splendor the grass of the field, which blooms today and is thrown on the fire tomorrow, will he not provide much more for you, O weak in faith.

So, do not worry and say, 'What are we to eat? or, What are we to drink?, or What are we to wear? All these things the pagans seek. Your heavenly father knows that you need them all. But seek first the kingdom (of God) and his righteousness, and all these things will be given you besides. Do not worry about tomorrow; tomorrow will take care of itself. Sufficient for a day is its own evil'« (Mt 6:24-34).

(Silence)

Be praised and glorified for ever, O my Lord, when you call me to you with such words. Yes, you are my master and teacher. I have no other, nor do I want to have one. I want to serve you and nobody else. Now here, before you I leave all my worries and anxiety, fear and mistrust. I present to you all that worries me, for it is hard to be bound and fettered, to be pensive and anxious. And you offer me, in your love, the freedom of birds and the beauty of lilies in the field.

Because of my own worries and plans I have no time for my friends, nor for anybody else. Could anybody give me a greater promise than yours, that you would take care of everything? O God, you want me to be like a child from morning till night, to live happily, in joy and in total abandonment, not worrying about anything.

After these words I still wonder whether it is possible at all. Yes, it is possible, for you say so, Jesus, and I shall understand it when you become my everything and when you are above all for me.

O Jesus, who would not give you glory, who would not adore you? I cannot but pray to you day and night. Jesus, if it is so, let me understand, so that you may always be my everything.

(Silence)

Our Father, Hail Mary, Glory Be

(Sing a hymn or meditate on the prayer of Jesus in Luke 22:41-44.)

»After withdrawing about a stone's throw from them and kneeling, he prayed, saying, 'Father, if you are willing, take this cup away from me; still, not my will but yours be done.' And to strengthen him an angel from heaven appeared to him. He was in such agony and he prayed so fervently that his sweat became like drops of blood falling on the ground« (Lk 22:41-44).

Have we trials or temptations? Is there trouble anywhere? We should never be discouraged. Take it to the Lord in prayer.

(From the song »What a Friend We Have In Jesus«)

6. Jesus, you said you had come because of the sinful and the sick. Thank you that in your holiness and excellence you do not turn away from us. Thank you for having forgiven me my sins and shared your bread with sinners. Thank you for not having feared the criticism of those who considered themselves righteous and despised others as sinful and unworthy. Therefore I am

praying to you now to forgive my sins, as well and to cleanse me completely.

Thank you, Jesus, for having sent out every Christian to be ready to do the same: to love without any conditions, especially where no reward is expected. Kneeling here before you, I decide for your way and ask you to make me worthy to pray in your name for my own cleansing and healing. Even more I thank you for being ready to heal others and bring them back to your friendship through me. Jesus, make me worthy.

Mary, Mother of every consolation, be with me now and pray with me that from this moment I may be whiter than snow and that I may be able to work for the benefit of all those for whom I now want to pray to your Son with you.

(Mention by name those you want to pray for. Remain in silence.)

Our Father, Hail Mary, Glory Be

Meditate on Psalms 103(102):8-10;13

»Merciful and gracious is the Lord, slow to anger and abounding in kindness. He will not always chide, nor does he keep his wrath forever. Not according to our sins does he deal with us, nor does he requite us according to our crimes. As a father has compassion on his

children, so the Lord has compassion on those who fear him...« (Ps 103(102):8-10; 13).

7. Jesus, now my heart is joyful. I know that you will take care of me and of all people, my brothers and sisters. At the end of this adoration I promise that from now on I shall care more for you and for your Word. I shall endeavor through prayer to experience your love and to pass it on. I know that my journey is still long, the destination still far. But thank you for the hope burning in my heart and for the love which has blazed up toward you, and at the same time toward my brothers and sisters.

Jesus, I pray to you, make your abode in me through Holy Communion. Grow and develop within me. Heal my soul and body. Keep me safe from every mental and physical illness, from every incurable and infectious disease.

Likewise, I beseech you to cure all the sick and the infirm. Glorify yourself in all of us. Let your face shine on the whole world through us.

Mary, be also with me. You are the Mother of Emmanuel, which means the Mother of God who decided to be with us forever.

Our Father, Hail Mary, Glory Be

(At the end, sing:)

Humbly let us voice our homage
For so great a sacrament;
Let all former rites surrender
To the Lord's New Testament;
What our senses fail to fathom,
Let us grasp through faith's consent.
Glory, honor, adoration
Let us sing with one accord.
Praised be God, almighty Father;
Praised be Christ, His Son, our Lord;
Praised be God the Holy Spirit;
Triune Godhead be adored. Amen.

V. You gave them bread from heaven.

R. Having all sweetness within it.

Let us pray.

O God, who in this wondrous sacrament has left us a memorial of your passion, grant us, we beseech you, so to venerate the sacred mysteries to your Body and Blood that we may perceive within us the effect of your redemption, who lives and reigns world without end.

R. Amen.

Blessed be God.

(Sing a closing song.)

PREPARATION, REALIZATION AND CONSEQUENCES OF THE FIRST EUCHARISTIC ENCOUNTER

(Based upon the experience of the disciples of Emmaus, the following is especially for those wanting to enter into the mystery of Adoration.)

Introductory Prayer

Heavenly Father, I ask you now in the name of your Son, Jesus Christ, to send me the Holy Spirit, so that my heart may be open and ready to accept your presence in Jesus Christ. You have sent him to us and he is our Emmanuel, God with us. Open our hearts Jesus, as you opened the hearts of the disciples on the way to Emmaus. You joined them. You went along with them as a stranger and as one who willingly listened to their lamentations, in order to open their hearts and to then reveal yourself. Then, the ice in their hearts melted, and they recognized you. Here I am, Jesus, and I ask you to do everything so that my heart can recognize your Word in this moment, be open for prayer and an encounter with you, so that after the prayer I shall be able to continue my way with you and with my human brothers in love. Amen.

(In silence present to Jesus your own situation and then pray:)

I believe in God the Father Almighty...

First Mystery: Jesus came closer to the disciples.

St. Luke writes:

»Now that very day two of them were going to a village seven miles from Jerusalem called Emmaus, and they were conversing about all the things that had occurred. And it happened that while they were conversing and debating, Jesus himself drew near and walked with them, but their eyes were prevented from recognizing him« (Lk 24:13-16).

Lord Jesus, thank you for not rejecting the disciples going to Emmaus. Although they had left Jerusalem and were going back home, you followed them. You did not leave them alone. You are the traveler with the travelers. You understood them, and therefore you joined them. Thank you.

Jesus, I now seriously ask myself about my life. You are also my fellow traveler, many times unrecognized, but a real fellow traveler. Can you get closer to me? What do I talk about with other people on my way? I must admit that I rarely talk about what happened to you, and very often my conversation turns into a discussion of other people's mistakes and their condemnation. Forgive me!

I understand that many times you followed me from a distance, and when you got closer, you could not participate in my conversation because my conversation was bad. Jesus, give me strength to overcome this evil within myself. Let my conversation always be accompanied by you, so that you can always take part in it. Let yourself be the topic of my conversation from now on, for you are my way and the light on my way.

Our Father, 10 Hail Marys, Glory Be, O My Jesus...

Second Mystery: They stopped, looking downcast.

St. Luke writes:

»He asked them, 'What are you discussing as you walk along?' They stopped, looking downcast. One of them, named Cleopas, said to him in reply, 'Are you the only visitor to Jerusalem who does not know of the things that have taken place there in these days?' And he replied to them, 'What sort of things?'« (Lk 24:17-19)

Jesus, your question surprised the two travelers. It is obvious that they loved you and they were sorry because you, as a »stranger,« did not know anything about the events. They did not even realize that you, with your resurrection, had already taken away the reason for their sorrow. Thank you, because you can and you want to stop sorrow and disappointments and turn them into new hope. Thank you for making that possible for me also.

Open our eyes in order to recognize the moments when I can and when I have to help others in your name. Forgive me, because many times I avoided sorrowful people, and many times I was afraid to accept despised people. I did not approach disappointed people, I did not reconcile those who were fighting. Forgive me and give me your Holy Spirit to be able to be your fellow traveler and a light to all those who are unhappy and in trouble. Jesus, be with me, and I will be a new person on the way of life with others.

Our Father, 10 Hail Marys, Glory Be, O my Jesus...

Third Mystery: But we were hoping.

St. Luke writes:

*»They said to him, 'The things that hap-
pened to Jesus the Nazarene, who was a
prophet mighty in deed and word before God
and all the people, how our chief priests and
rulers both handed him over to a sentence of
death and crucified him. But we were hoping
that he would be the one to redeem Israel...'«*
(Lk 24:19b-21).

Jesus! The disciples had been with you
for some time. You taught them. You talked
to them about the death and the resurrection. But they did not understand anything.
They remained strangers, although they
were close to you. Their faith stopped at
death. They knew that you were a great
prophet by words and by deeds, and because of that they had hoped. But their hope
failed, because with their faith they were not
able to understand the meaning of the
Cross, death, the tomb and the resurrection.

Jesus, you know that my faith is weak.
Because of that my hope is not strong. Wake
up my faith, widen my faith so that my hope
in you will no longer be shaky. I will be able
to say together with St. Paul: »I knew whom
I trusted! Send me the Holy Spirit.«

Jesus, I plead for all those who are disappointed in people. Change life in the family
where parents are disappointed with their

children, because their unfulfilled hopes have become the source of conflict. Change us and direct our hope!

Our Father, 10 Hail Marys, Glory Be, O my Jesus...

Fourth Mystery: Was it not necessary to suffer?

St. Luke writes:

»And he said to them, 'Oh, how foolish you are! How slow of heart to believe all that the prophets spoke! Was it not necessary that the Messiah should suffer these things and enter into his glory?' Then beginning with Moses and all the prophets, he interpreted to them what referred to him in all the scriptures« (Lk 24:25-27).

Jesus! It was not easy even for you to suffer, but you said that you would have to suffer. And you did. But, Jesus, who can prove to the innocent that innocent ones would have to suffer? Who will tell those who are deprived of their rights that they will achieve their rights by means of suffering? Who will be able to prove to innocent children, killed in their mother's womb, that it had to be so? You do not remain speechless in front of the victims of violence, Jesus, and you turn the fate of all those who suffer into the glory of resurrection.

Let the crosses of all those who suffer blossom with the hope and the joy of the resurrection, so that they can be clothed with peace and feed themselves with the honey and the milk of new justice. Help us to be able to carry our cross as you did, with love, even when we do not understand them. Mary, Mother of all those who suffer, do not leave us in our suffering, as you did not leave your Son.

Our Father, 10 Hail Marys, Glory Be, O my Jesus...

Fifth Mystery: Did our hearts not burn?

St. Luke writes:

»As they approached the village to which they were going, he gave them the impression that he was going on farther. But they urged him, 'Stay with us, for it is nearly evening and the day is almost over.' So he went in to stay with them. And it happened that, while he was with them at table, he took bread, said the blessing, broke it, and gave it to them. With that their eyes were opened and they recognized him, but he vanished from their sight. Then they said to each other, 'Were not our hearts burning [within us] while he spoke to us on the way and opened the scriptures to us?'«

Jesus, in this mystery, I plead for all those who proclaim the Word. Give them your Spirit and inspire their word. Let them proclaim your Word in order to warm cold hearts, to soften hard hearts, to turn hearts that curse into hearts that will praise and glorify you, to turn the desperate hearts into hearts of hope, and to turn sorrowful hearts into joyful hearts.

I especially plead for those messengers of your Word who are sorrowful and lonely, for those who wonder why they have been called and for those who have abandoned their vocation. Please give them the grace to celebrate Holy Mass so that they may always be able to recognize you in the Holy Eucharist. I personally plead for all those who receive Holy Communion, so that they may be able to recognize you and never forget you.

On behalf of all people, I pray that you stay with us and give us the abundance of your graces.

Our Father, 10 Hail Marys, Glory Be, O my Jesus...

Final Prayer

Lord Jesus, thank you for this encounter. Be the remedy for my soul and the protection for my life. From today on, like your disciples after the meeting with you, I want to go into my life more decidedly and not to run away from my duties. May you and your Mother always be my fellow travelers. Amen.

ADORATION OF THE HOLY CROSS

In the name of the Father, and of the Son, and of the Holy Spirit. Amen.

We adore you, O Christ, and we bless you; because by your Holy Cross, you have redeemed the world.

1. Jesus, I fall on my knees before your cross, the cross on which you died out of love for me. By it you obtained eternal salvation in heaven for us, and opened the way of peace and reconciliation on earth. Thank you for your cross. Thank you for having carried it with love.

Jesus, I admit to you right away that I do not understand why you had to suffer. Therefore, all the greater is my gratitude to you for your cross. Thank you for having marked me with the sign of the cross from the very beginning. At baptism this sign of salvation was indelibly imprinted into my soul and heart. Although I do not understand your cross, it is neither a folly nor a scandal for me, but a sign of your love and the way of my salvation.

Jesus, your Mother, brave and faithful, was standing under your cross. She was listening and taking to heart the words you

143

uttered at the moment of your terrible passion and death.

Mary, thank you for having carried the cross yourself. Thank you for having called me to stand by the cross and before the cross and to devote myself to it.

»Dear children: I want to tell you that the cross should be in the center these days. Pray especially before the cross, from which great graces come. Now make a special consecration to the cross in your homes. Promise that you will not offend Jesus, or the cross and inflict insults on Him. Thank you for having responded to my call« (September 12, 1985).

Here, Mary, at the beginning of this adoration, at your word, I devote myself to the cross. Be with me now and let this devotion be complete.

O cross, I consecrate myself to you. I renounce every sin against you and every sin in the world. I renounce every insult I have inflicted and which others have inflicted. I am ashamed, Jesus, of having sinned, of having offended you and the sign of my personal salvation. But from today I belong only to your cross. Let it be the only sign of hope and salvation for me.

144

(Silence in front of the cross.)

Our Father, Hail Mary, Glory be...

(While reading the text of Isaiah 53:2-4, look at the cross.)

»He grew up like a sapling before him, like a shoot from the parched earth. There was in him no stately bearing to make us look at him, nor appearance that would attract us to him. He was spurned and avoided by men, a man of suffering, accustomed to infirmity. One of those from whom men hide their faces, spurned, and we held him in no esteem. Yet it was our infirmities that he bore, our sufferings that he endured, while we thought of him as stricken, as one smitten by God and afflicted« (Is 53:2-4).

(Sing the following hymn.)

Cross of Jesus we adore you,
Our whole life we give to you,
We dearly love you.

2. Jesus, your cross is not a mute sign, but a cry for forgiveness, a cry for reconciliation of men to God the Father, a cry for universal justice and love. You were not silent on the cross. Your suffering did not close your mouth nor twist it with revenge, but rather, you spoke at the hardest moment and sought forgiveness and love.

So, thank you for having pronounced the words of forgiveness when you most had a reason to condemn. Thank you for having asked your Father for forgiveness and mercy at the time of crucifixion.

Father, thank you for having heard the words of your Son, when your fatherly goodness was »tested« because of the Son's suffering. Thank you, Father for his having pronounced the words:

»Father, forgive them; they do not know what they are doing.«

Jesus, none of the men, especially those who were preparing your death, had expected such words. Misled by hatred and endless darkness, they vented their anger on you by nailing you to the cross. They made fun of you. And you prayed to the Father not to punish them for their deeds.

Let these words now echo in my heart.

(Keep repeating to yourself: »Father, forgive them; they do not know what they are doing.«)

Jesus, scenes of cruelty are vivid in my mind. What cruelty of men! You did only good and this is how you were repaid. I am sorry that something like this could happen. Grant me tears that I may start crying before your cross, which is a sign of our human cruelty and attraction to evil, but even more a sign of your love for us.

Mary, you also experienced all this and heard His words of forgiveness. Thank you for having appeared to our visionaries with a cross in your hand, crying and repeating the words: »Peace, peace, peace.«

I want these words to echo in my heart now. Let them inspire repentance and the desire for reconciliation in me.

(Remain in deep meditation and repent of your sins, especially the hatred and intolerance around you.)

Jesus, through Mary, grant that I may receive the grace of forgiving. Forgive me both when I know and when I do not know what I am doing. Cure me of my wickedness so that peace and forgiveness may enter deeply into me.

(Silence)

Our Father, Hail Mary, Glory be...

(Sing or meditate on Psalms 130(129):1-5.)

»Out of the depths I cry to you, O Lord; Lord, hear my voice. Let your ears be attentive to my voice in supplication. If you, O Lord, mark iniquities, Lord, who can stand? But with you is

forgiveness, that you may be revered. I trust in the Lord; my soul trusts in his word« (Ps 130(129):1-5).

> Forgive me, my God, I repent, forgive me.
> Look, in sorrow my heart is dying.

3. Jesus, in your cross I see your endless love. You gave everything for us, for your brothers and sisters. You loved us even to the point of a humiliating death. You entered into the deepest levels of human suffering. You suffered endlessly. Although you carried the cross with love, you were not spared deep pain. I cannot say that it was easy for you to forgive because you are the Son of God. It was not easy for you either, for you suffered without consolation, and that is the hardest form of suffering. You felt forsaken, lonely, helpless. That is why you uttered that soul stirring cry, »My God, my God, why have you forsaken me?«

Jesus, let these words enter deeply into my heart. Let them penetrate into the depths of my consciousness and subconsciousness. Let them wake me up and inspire full love and abandonment to the Father, for you emptied the cup of loneliness on my behalf.

(Keep repeating these words in silence.)

Jesus, forgive me that my love is not unconditional. Forgive me for having only sought my consolation and for having often so easily cried out to the Father, »Where are you, why do you not help, why do you not hear me?« Forgive my distrust of the Father. So shallow and rootless is my word, »Father, your Will be done.«

Jesus, I pray to you for all those who are crying and moaning in their pain now. They do not doubt the Father's love but, resigned to His will, drink the cup of suffering and present it for the salvation of the world. Let love and trust grow in them through their trials and tests.

Jesus, I pray to you also for all who have lost trust in the Father because of suffering, and now do not pray nor seek the Father's will, but live embittered, unreconciled to the Father and to men. Jesus, you experienced suffering. So you do not condemn them but present their cries to the Father, asking Him to forgive them, to appease them.

Mary, Mother of consolation, at the moment of deep suffering you could not offer consolation to your Son. You were helpless yourself, though not desperate, but repeated the words once said in Nazareth, »I am the servant of the Lord, let it be done to me as you say.« Mary, when we do not know how to or cannot accept the Father's will, when we feel forsaken and misunderstood, be near our cross and say in place of us, »Father, here I am. I belong to you. I am yours.«

(Silence)

Our Father, Hail Mary, Glory be...

(Meditate on Psalms 34(33):18-20 or sing a hymn.)

»When the just cry out, the Lord hears them, and from all their distress he rescues them. The Lord is close to the brokenhearted; and those who are crushed in spirit he saves. Many are the troubles of the just man, but out of them all the Lord delivers him...« (Ps 34(33):18-20).

> You have given me gifts without number,
> But, alas, I am a careless creature.

4. Father, before the cross of your Son Jesus Christ I give you thanks for all his words from the cross. I know you heard them.

Mary, thank you for having accepted your new mission so wholeheartedly when Jesus said to you, »Woman, there is your son.« Thank you that your heart had grown so ripe in love through suffering and pain so that your Son, at the moment of His death, entrusted to you all those he had given his life for on the cross. In this way, Mary, you gave birth to all of us under the cross. O brave Mother, thank you for not having feared pain and the cross. Thank you for having deserved such confidence.

(Remain in silence and listen in your heart to Jesus' words: »Woman, there is your son.«)

My Jesus, what a consolation it must have been for you that your Mother bore patiently her cross following you on your way to the cross. Now I pray to you for all who are lonely, who have become withdrawn, who have nobody, or who have been abandoned.

Jesus, I pray to you especially for the children who have been abandoned by their parents, who in their selfishness forgot those they had given life to. I also pray to you before the cross for the children killed by their mothers before they were born. Mary, be a Mother to all. I know that you are faithful and will not run away, that you are courageous. I know that you will always find a word of consolation in suffering, a word of joy at the moment of sorrow, and a word of light at the moment of darkness. And I know, when you are not able to say the word, you will still be a Mother, for you took your Son's words seriously. Therefore, thank you also for the following words:

»**Dear children: I, your Mother, love you and want to encourage you to prayer. I am tireless, dear children, and keep calling you even when you are far from my heart. I am a Mother, and although I feel pain for each who has gone astray, I forgive easily and I am happy about each child that turns to me. Thank you for having responded to my call**« (November 14, 1985).

Our Father, Hail Mary, Glory be...

Under the cross the Mother stood
Watching her Son nailed to the wood,
With bitter tears in her eyes.

(Be consoled by this text of Luke 23:27-29.)

»*A large crowd of people followed Jesus, including many women who mourned and lamented him. Jesus turned to them and said, "Daughters of Jerusalem, do not weep for me; weep instead for yourselves and for your children, for indeed, the days are coming when people will say, 'Blessed are the barren, the wombs that never bore and the breasts that never nursed...'"*« (Lk 23:27-29).

152

5. Jesus, you did not become blind in suffering, nor did hatred close your eyes, because your love and the sense of mission were divinely strong. You did not fall into darkness, because the divine light you bore in your life was stronger than darkness. Thank you, therefore, even more now for having taken care of a disciple, and through him, all of us, when you said: »Woman, there is your son.«

How beautiful and moving are these words which you addressed to the disciple you loved in a special way, asking him to take care of your Mother, now his Mother. O how did these words echo in the ears of your beloved disciple, now your brother. What else could he do when you said, »There is your mother,« but say in his heart with joy, with deep sense of responsibility and with gratitude: »Yes, she is my Mother.« So from that hour onward he took her into his care.

My Jesus, I can hardly imagine what a deep bond of love and togetherness was established and made firm between you, your Mother and your disciple at that moment. Thank you for having consciously realized the Father's plan. With the cross and under the cross, the beginning of a new mankind was realized.

Mary, thank you for having accepted your new son, John, and in him all of us. John, thank you for having accepted Mary as your Mother in our name from that moment onward. Mary, I accept you, too.

(Silence)

I know that a bond, born in suffering, is stronger than any blood relationship. Therefore, Jesus, I pray to you now for all our families where the links between parents and children, between brothers and sisters have broken, where unity has disappeared.

(Pray for a family you know is in difficulty.)

I pray to you, Jesus, also for all our monastic communities, for all spiritual movements, and for the whole Church. Let our spiritual communities be born and renewed by the strength of togetherness born in suffering.

Our Father, Hail Mary, Glory be...

In your heart there is enough space for all people,

For you have come to all, that all may come to love you.

(Meditate on the text of Hosea 2:21-22.)

»I will espouse you to me forever: I will espouse you in right and in justice, in love and

in mercy; I will espouse you in fidelity, and you shall know the Lord« (Hos 2:21-22).

6. Jesus, divine sufferer, you are bringing to an end your deed of salvation on the cross, your mission. You finished it in the midst of the deepest pain and the rage of evil and sin. All the rage of hell, all the darkness of the world has come down upon you, but you remained divinely dignified and could say, »Now it is finished. Father, into your hands I commend my spirit.« The Father received your spirit. And after the horrible cry on the cross, the door of heaven is open again to all who want it, even to the criminal on the cross. Thank you, my divine brother and friend, for having taken upon yourself such pain and agony for my sake. Jesus, let your death cry arouse my consciousness and subconsciousness so that I may tear myself away from evil and sin, from dissolute living and hatred, from darkness and hell, and be open to the light.

Mary, obtain by prayer this grace for me. I remain with you, Mary, in silence.

Jesus, I pray to you with Mary for my death's hour. Even now I consciously declare: »Father, into your hands I commend my spirit.« As early as now, Father, I give over to you my pain and fear of my meeting with you at that moment. Cleanse me that I may be able to meet you. Jesus, on that day take me to your kingdom, as you did that criminal from the cross.

(Pray in silence.)

Jesus, I pray to you for those who are now at death's hour and are going through a deep fear of leaving this world and of facing you. Show them your love. Curtail their earthly sufferings which breed despair, and turn them into hope. Have mercy on the dying, you who died so devoutly. Mary, be with every dying person as you were with your dying son. Alleviate their pain of loneliness by your gentle motherly presence.

Jesus, I also pray to you for those who are now sad, worried or disappointed because they are going to part with their dear ones. Open for them the gracious fountain of faith and hope. I especially pray to you, Jesus, for mothers who hold a sick child in their arms, at its last breath. Be a consoler to them with your Mother Mary.

> Our Father, Hail Mary, Glory be, Eternal rest...

> When my body is dead and still,
> Let my soul with your glory fill
> To enjoy you for ever.

(Meditate on Psalms 65(64):4-6 or sing.)

»To you all flesh must come because of wicked deeds. We are overcome by our sins; it is you who pardon them. Happy is the man you choose and bring to dwell in your courts. May we be filled with the good things of your house, the holy things of your temple. With awe-inspiring deeds of justice you answer us, O God our savior, the hope of all the ends of the earth and of the distant seas« (Ps 65(64):4-6).

7. Jesus, they slashed and tortured your entire body, but darkness and sin could not affect your spirit and soul. Now, in front of your cross, I am standing personally, wounded in soul and body, and I am asking you for healing.

On the cross you forgave me. You said: »Father, forgive them; they do not know what they are doing.«

It is only an offer to me. It is not yet a received grace. For, as the penitent thief went to heaven, the other cursed the offer of forgiveness. Therefore, Jesus, I want to seek, and I am seeking, not only forgiveness but also the healing of my wickedness: »Jesus, Son of David, have mercy on me.«

My heart is restless. It seeks everything, yet has the least time to be before you. It is restless because it does not understand

157

your love. Move my heart that it may no longer wander but find inspiration in you who, by forgiving, opened an inexhaustible source of peace. Jesus, Son of David, have mercy on me and cure me of restlessness.

I know that you are the Master. You can do everything. You lowered yourself to be closer to me. And I do not feel it. I remain cold and so easily offend you. O, cure me of bad tendencies. Jesus, Son of David, have mercy on me and cure me.

What discontent, revenge, ill humor and mousiness exist in me. How hard it is for me to forget insults. I bear a limitless revengefulness, and make life difficult for myself. O, cure me of all my bitterness with your mildness. Jesus, Son of David, have mercy on me.

O Jesus, hanging on the cross, you prayed for me, too. But I have forgotten prayer in distress so many times and have instead blasphemed, cursed and despaired, for I have no strength to retreat to prayer. Forgive me. Cure me. Teach me to pray. Jesus, Son of David, have mercy on me.

It is not only I who am unhappy on this earth. Around me I see so many unhappy, dissatisfied people, involved in quarrels and conflicts. They often blame only you. But they cannot see their sin as the cause of their unhappiness, and so are not converted. It is individuals, families, monastic communities, the world who are unhappy. O Jesus, cure us all. Cure parents, and cure the souls and hearts of the young, heal all the wounds which sin has inflicted. Jesus, Son of David, have mercy on us.

Jesus, cure me of every deafness. I especially ask you to cure me of deafness to the Word you send me through your Mother. Cure my parish community of the deafness. Jesus, Son of David, have mercy on us.

Prayer for Physical Healing

(May be added before the final blessing.)

Jesus, your hands and feet were pierced. Your side was pierced only that you may cure us, that you may heal our bodies which were created as the temples of the Holy Spirit. Jesus, cure us by your patience in suffering: cure the sick and their attendants of impatience. You know that patience is easily lost in suffering. Heal our love so that we may bear pain as you did. Jesus, Son of David, have mercy on us.

Jesus, you accepted a crown of thorns on your head. You received blows. By your wounds and the crown of thorns cure me of every headache. Jesus, Son of David, have mercy on me.

You closed your eyes in order to restore our sight. Heal my eyes. Restore sight to the blind. Jesus, Son of David, cure me of my blindness.

Jesus, you were obedient to the Father. You heard his word and you glorified him with your lips. Jesus, restore our hearing and speech. Heal the deaf and mute. Jesus, Son of David, have mercy on us.

Jesus, by your pierced hands and feet cure every paralysis. Cure the hands which are clenched into fists. Jesus, Son of David, have mercy on us.

Jesus, they pierced your chest and heart so that you might cure us. Heal our sick hearts, our bad blood circulation, our sick blood. Heal gout. Jesus, Son of David, have mercy on us.

You suffered innocently. Therefore, I pray to you for all those who suffer because of other people's inattentiveness, because others are stronger and without love. Heal them, Jesus, Son of David, and have mercy on them.

If it be the Father's will that my suffering and illness should remain, then I accept them now again, and ask for strength for me and for all sufferers. Jesus, Son of David, have mercy on us.

Mary, here we are by the cross with you. You know our woes, our problems and pains. You know our anguish and physical suffering. O Mother of consolation, thank you that I am not alone. Thank you for your being with me in my crosses and sufferings. I stretch out my hand to you and devote my life to you so that I may remain by the cross of your Son.

Mother, you said to us:

»**Dear children: I want to clothe you, day by day, in holiness, goodness, obedience and love of God, that you may, with each day, become more beautiful and more prepared for your Master. Dear children: Obey and live my messages. I want to lead you. Thank you for having responded to my call**« (October 24, 1985).

Mary, clothe us as a mother does and prepare us, wash and clean us that we may be ready for our Master and for each other.

Our Father, Hail Mary, Glory be...

And the blessing of peace, love and
     mercy,
The blessing of spiritual and physical
     health
May descend from the cross now on me
And on the whole world.

In the name of the Father...

THE WAY OF THE CROSS

Opening Prayer

Jesus, you prayed in the Garden of Gethsemane.

Heavenly Father, you sent your Son to us to save the world. Thank you for thinking about us with your love and thank you for taking care of us. With the life, suffering, and death of your Son on the Cross, you opened for us a door to a new life, and pulled us out from under our debt. Thank you.

Thank you Jesus, thank you for accepting in obedience the will of our Father. Now I am watching you in the Garden of Gethsemane. You prayed by yourself. You urged the apostles to pray and to keep vigil, but still they fell asleep. You understood them, you did not condemn them. You said: »It's true, the Spirit is willing, but the flesh is weak.« Mary, your Mother, was not present. Had she been, she surely would not have fallen asleep. She would have kept vigil with you. Her love would not have let her fall asleep, while you sweat blood and suffered in your prayer. Jesus, although you were abandoned by people, you still prayed to your Father to be saved from torments, suffering, and the bitter cup. Thank you for your firmness out of which these words were born: »Father, your will be done.« At that moment the angel came to console you, to replenish you. The suffering had begun and you accepted it. You repeated the words your Mother said at the moment of your conception: »I am the servant of the Lord. Be it done to me according to thy Word.«

Jesus, I am sorry that the apostles slept, that their bodies were so weak. I am sorry Mary was not present. Therefore, I am even more grateful to you for the immeasurable love that you have shown us.

Forgive me also for your having to tell me over and over again: »Pray, do not doze off, do not sleep. Pray so that you will not be tempted.« And so many times I only heard your words in my dreams, and remained exposed to temptations. Forgive me. From now on, I want to pray and keep vigil with you. I will not leave you alone again. I am deciding to keep vigil with you. Now I remain silent and repeat these words in my heart for you: »Father, your will be done.«

(After a pause, I continue to pray.)

Jesus, I present to you all those who are now struggling in a mortal battle, who are fighting all kinds of temptations. I pray to you for all those ready to do the will of our Father, in spite of all their difficulties. I pray for all those of your disciples who sleep and day dream, because they are overcome by sin. I pray to you for all the sick, lonely, and persecuted, for all those in mortal battle. In the name of all of them I say to you: »Father, your will be done.«

(Remain silent, and after a short pause continue praying.)

Jesus, Judas came and betrayed you in the garden. He betrayed you with the kiss of a friend. How difficult it must have been for you. Those who wanted to be with you, they slept; and the one who betrayed you did not sleep, he was always awake. I am sorry it had to be that way. Forgive those who sleep, who do not make a move, who remain asleep in their betrayals. Thank you for forgiving those who betrayed you because they decided against you. Forgive me, forgive all of us for our kisses of betrayal, for all of our insincere words.

Jesus, with all my heart and soul, I am going to awaken my spirit, and I will follow you on your way. Your will be done. Amen.

(Now start to pray the Stations of the Cross as they are offered in this book.)

Introductory Prayer

Jesus, your Mother has called us to meditate on your passion and death, to honor your cross. I am ready to follow you with your Mother and mine on your way of the cross with the love with which your Mother once followed you. I want to bear my crosses as you once did yours. Grant that by your example, I may learn how to help others to bear their crosses and to rise after each fall.

Mary, I begin now with you, to follow Jesus on the way of the cross. I am carrying my cross, the cross of my family, of the Church and the world. I want to shoulder every cross and to help everybody. You said to the members of the Medugorje parish: »You parishioners have a big and heavy cross, but do not be afraid of carrying it. My Son is there to help you.« I am sure you meant these words for me, too, in order to encourage me. Thank you. Amen.

The First Station

Jesus, Pilate condemns you to death.

We adore you, O Christ, and we bless you;
Because by your Holy Cross, you have redeemed the world.

»Pilate then summoned the chief priests, the rulers, and the people and said to them, 'You brought this man to me and accused him of inciting the people to revolt. I have conducted my investigation in your presence and have not found this man guilty of the charges you have brought against him...'« (Lk 23:14).

»The just man perishes, but no one takes it to heart. Devout men are swept away, with no one giving it a thought. Though he is taken away from the presence of evil, the just man enters into peace. Of whom do you make sport, at whom do you open with your mouth, and put out your tongue? Are you not rebellious children, a worthless race?« (Is 57:1-4).

»For Christ also suffered for sins once, the righteous for the sake of the unrighteous, that he might lead you to God. Put to death in the flesh, he was brought to life in the spirit« (1 Pt 3:18).

Jesus, here I am now in front of you. You do not condemn me, you do not seek my guilt but want to wash me of it. Thank you. Now I am sincerely sorry for having condemned others so many times, spoken badly about my neighbors, for having passed over in silence the injustices and wrongs done to others.

Jesus, grant that from now on I may be completely yours. I pray to you also for all those who do the devotions of the way of the cross, climbing Križevac, or in their churches or homes. Be merciful to them all. Take away the condemnations that bear on them and those they have inflicted upon others. From now on let us stand in front of each other, like brother in front of brother or sister in front of sister. Do not let the just perish any more. Let love and peace come to reign.

Mary, you heard the condemnation but did not condemn. Stand by my side and by the side of all your sons and daughters. Thank you for having said:

»Dear children: This evening I would like to invite you in a special way to perseverance in trials. Think how the Almighty suffers because of your sins even today. So when sufferings come, present them as a sacrifice to God. Thank you for having responded to my call« (March 29, 1984).

(After a short silence present your crosses and sufferings to God.)
Our Father, Hail Mary, Glory be...
Have mercy on us, O Lord.
Have mercy on us.

The Second Station

Jesus, you take the cross upon your
shoulders.

We adore you, O Christ, and we bless
you;
Because by your Holy Cross, you have
redeemed the world.

*»So they took Jesus, and carrying the cross
himself he went out to what is called the Place
of the Skull, in Hebrew, Golgotha« (Jn 19:17).*

*»Yet it was our infirmities that he bore, our
sufferings that he endured, while we thought of
him as stricken, as one smitten by God and
afflicted...« (Is 53:4). »We had all gone astray
like sheep, each following his own way; but the
Lord laid upon him the guilt of us all. Though
he was harshly treated, he submitted and
opened not his mouth; like a lamb led to the
slaughter or a sheep before the shearers, he
was silent and opened not his mouth« (Is 53:6-
7). »Then he said to all, 'If anyone wishes to
come after me, he must deny himself and take
up his cross daily and follow me. For whoever
wishes to save his life will lose it, but whoever
loses his life for my sake will save it...« (Lk
9:23-24).*

Jesus, you voluntarily took up your
cross, because such was the Father's will at
that moment. You allowed yourself to be

treated harshly so that we might avoid ill-treatment. I am sorry for having so many times shaken off my cross, choosing the easier way. I am sorry for having often evaded the cross of love and patience, and chosen the crosses of unreconciliation, hatred, selfishness, and impatience. Now, I realize that with my behavior I have often imposed heavy crosses on the shoulders of my neighbors. Forgive me. From now on I am willing to accept crosses the way you did. Now I forgive all those who, with their sins, burdened me so many times with heavy, too heavy crosses. I pray to you for those who insulted me, who did not love me, who did not forgive me my weaknesses and sins, but repaid my weaknesses and offenses with evil. I forgive them. Please, forgive them, too.

Mary, now I understand better that you are with me. Obtain grace for me through your prayers that I may know how to accept and carry crosses. Thank you for having urged me to pray for love in sufferings:

»**Dear children: In these days, while you are glorifying the cross joyfully, I would like your cross to be a joy for you. Pray especially, dear children, that you may accept sickness and sufferings with**

love the way Jesus did. Only in this way shall I be able to grant you readily the graces and healings which Jesus allows me. Thank you for having responded to my call« (September 11, 1986).

Mary, do not tire of teaching me how to accept and carry crosses.

Our Father, Hail Mary, Glory be...
Have mercy on us, O Lord.
Have mercy on us.

The Third Station

Jesus, you fall the first time under the cross.

We adore you, O Christ, and we bless you;
Because by your Holy Cross, you have redeemed the world.

»*To the weak I became weak, to win over the weak. I have become all things to all, to save at least some*« (1 Cor 9:22).

»*When it was evening, they brought him many who were possessed by demons and he drove out the spirits by a word and cured all the sick, to fulfill what had been said by Isaiah the prophet: 'He took away our infirmities and bore our diseases'*« (Mt 8:16-17).

171

Jesus, I am watching how you have fallen under the cross. I know that even voluntary crosses can become too heavy. You need not have fallen. You could have called hosts of angels and you would not have fallen. But you went the way of a suffering man. You became like us in all things but sin. Thank you, Jesus.

When I think now of the falls of my love, faith and hope, I can only say: »Forgive me.« So many times have I put aside my cross and have not wanted to carry it, so that others had to fall under it. Forgive me that my love has been short of breath so many times. My faith and hope have often given way to despair, also.

Jesus, thank you for not having given up your way after the fall. Thank you for not having said to the Father: »I cannot any longer,« but you rose and went on. Jesus, give me strength that I might rise after every fall. Watch over me so that I will not fall again.

I pray to you also for those I passed by and was not ready to help get out of their troubles. Jesus, grant them the favor to rise, and teach me to help others rise.

My Savior, many from the whole world have stood in front of this station, making decisions to take care not to fall. Now they are again crushed by the crosses of suffering, sin and evil. Jesus, may your mercy find them and help them to their feet.

Peace in the world has fallen under the burden of hatred. Justice and love have fallen under the burden of the anxiety for money and possessions. Many are so tied down to material goods that they do not care to rise. Jesus, you fell for all that they might rise. Grant that we may all rise and proceed on the way of resurrection.

(Pray by name for someone whom you think is in great trouble.)

Mary, you helplessly watched the fall of your Son. But your presence and your faithfulness were certainly a great consolation to him. Thank you for promising to be with us, too:

»**Dear children: No, you do not know how much grace God is giving you. You do not want to be moved these days, when the Holy Spirit is acting in a special way. Your hearts are turned to earthly things, and they engross you. Turn your hearts to prayer and ask for the outpouring of the Holy Spirit on you. Thank you for having responded to my call**« (May 9, 1985).

Mary, move us that we may rise with our crosses and be healed by the fall of your Son.

> Our Father, Hail Mary, Glory be...
> Have mercy on us, O Lord.
> Have mercy on us.

The Fourth Station

Jesus, you meet your faithful Mother Mary.

We adore you, O Christ, and we bless you;
Because by your Holy Cross, you have redeemed the world.

»Come, all you who pass by the way, look and see whether there is any suffering like my suffering, which has been dealt me when the Lord afflicted me on the day of his blazing wrath...« (Lam 1:12). »He left me desolate, in pain all the day...« (Lam 1:13). »At this I weep, my eyes run with tears: far from me are all who could console me, and who might revive me...« (Lam 1:16).

»Behold, this child is destined for the fall and rise of many in Israel, and to be a sign that will be contradicted (and you yourself a sword will pierce) so that the thoughts of many hearts may be revealed« (Lk 2:34-35).

Mary, you met your Son on the Way of the Cross. All you could do was to give Him a consoling look. You certainly could see in His eyes that He had accepted the suffering and the cross to save us. Mary, thank you for not having withdrawn. Love was stronger than bitterness and when your eyes met, you both accepted the Father's will again. You both suffered and carried the cross in love and devotion. Mary, obtain for me by prayer, faithfulness like yours.

Jesus, forgive me for having avoided meetings with you, forgive me that they have often been superficial. Give me the grace of meeting you on every occasion.

I would like to meet others with love, too, both when I am suffering myself and when they are suffering. I do not want to run away from anybody again. Jesus, I also pray to you for all the people who are suffering yet do not meet anybody who would be willing to help. I pray to you for all who are despised.

Jesus, I also pray to you for all those who perform these devotions on Križevac. Let them meet you. Please meet them, too. Let their life change and their sufferings turn for their good and for the glory of the Father.

Mary, you have attracted many people to Križevac. Accompany them on their way as you did your Son. Let your motherly look meet each pilgrim that each may return home comforted and continue on life's course in hope.

Thank you for the warning:

»Dear children: No, you do not know how to love and you do not know how to listen with love to the words I am giving you. Be aware, my dear ones, that I am your Mother and that I have come to earth in order to teach you to listen out of love, to pray out of love, and not because and when you are forced to by crosses. It is through a cross that God is glorified in every man. Thank you for having responded to my call« (November 29, 1984).

Mary, I decide to learn again to carry the cross with love and to meet with love those bearing their crosses.

> Our Father, Hail Mary, Glory be...
> Have mercy on us, O Lord.
> Have mercy on us.

The Fifth Station

Jesus, Simon of Cyrene helps you carry the cross.

We adore you, O Christ, and we bless you;
Because by your Holy Cross, you have redeemed the world.

»As they led him away they took hold of a certain Simon, a Cyrenean, who was coming in from the country; and after laying the cross on him, they made him carry it behind Jesus« (Lk 23:26).

»But rejoice to the extent that you share in the sufferings of Christ, so that when his glory is revealed you may also rejoice exultantly. If you are insulted for the name of Christ, blessed are you, for the Spirit of glory and of God rests upon you« (1 Pt 4:13-14).

My Jesus, those who had the task to torture you as much as possible and to crucify you as soon as possible, looked for somebody to help you carry the cross. And they forced Simon, a man coming to the temple for the Passover, into carrying your cross.

Simon, how did you feel? Did you not murmur to yourself: »Why do I have to carry the cross for somebody who, according to our law, has deserved it? Do I have to share

177

His disgrace?« Simon, I understand your having resisted and murmured. But you still helped carry the cross for the one who knew how to find a way to say thank you. You helped Jesus carry the cross. We all call you blessed Simon, for Jesus certainly rewarded you with eternal life, and for that Jesus, thank you for having accepted Simon's help.

Let me recognize you, Jesus, in every suffering man. Let me understand how I can be more blessed than Simon of Cyrene because I can help you every day. Help me make use of every opportunity, so that I may enjoy the happiness of love even here on earth.

Jesus, I pray to you for all those I have not wanted to help in their trouble. Forgive me, and cure them of their inflicted wounds.

Thank you for those whom I have helped in your name and who have helped me in your name. I pray to you also for all those who readily help today, because they love you and in you their brothers and sisters.

Jesus, many perform the Way of the Cross here and look for a Simon. Let them feel how close you are to them and let them go back home ready to carry each other's crosses and to share your sufferings in this way.

Mary, thank you for your readiness to teach me to recognize and to love every human being as a brother or a sister. Thank you for reassuring me that I can help Jesus even today:

»Dear children: I invite you to help Jesus with your prayers to realize all the plans which he is making here. Present your sacrifices to Jesus as well, so that everything may be realized as he has planned it, thus thwarting all the plans of Satan. Thank you for having responded to my call« (January 9, 1986).

Mary, with you do I present my prayers, and my sacrifices, and my life for the realization of the plans for love and peace in the world.

Our Father, Hail Mary, Glory be...
Have mercy on us, O Lord.
Have mercy on us.

The Sixth Station

Jesus, Veronica wipes your face.

We adore you, O Christ, and we bless you;

Because by your Holy Cross, you have
redeemed the world.

*»Fairer in beauty are you than the sons of
men« (Ps 45:2).*

*»There was in him no stately bearing to
make us look at him, nor appearance that
would attract us to him. He was spurned and
avoided by men, a man of suffering, accustomed to infirmity, one of those from whom
men hide their faces, spurned, and we held
him in no esteem« (Is 53:2-3).*

*»Answer me speedily, O Lord, my breath is
at an end. Hide not your face from me, lest I
should become like those going down into the
pit« (Ps 143:7). »Let your countenance shine
upon your servant...« (Ps 119:135).*

Jesus, they also deformed your face.
Blood mixed with sweat. You could not be
recognized any more. Your heart was the
most beautiful, that is why your face was
beautiful. You were shining with your inner
beauty even at the hour of contempt and
humiliation.

And then a courageous woman meets you
and wipes your face. Jesus, you did not
forget to be grateful. Veronica found your
face impressed on her handkerchief.

Amid all the hostility toward you, not
everyone forgot that had been only goodness, that so many times you had stopped

the tears of bitterness and anguish, tears that resulted from pain and suffering. Thank you, Veronica, for not having been afraid, although you were likely to meet with personal insults and humiliations because you had helped a condemned person.

Jesus, I am sorry for having so many times disfigured my own face and the faces of others with my sins, even knowing that you identified yourself with us all. That means that I did the same to your face. Forgive me, Jesus. You wanted my face and my life to be a reflection of your face and your life. But I have forgotten it so many times, so that your light and your joy could not reach others. Please, clean my face of every stain and wrinkle that your light may shine forth from me, too.

I pray to you also for all those who had looked up to me for more love and understanding, but my look was obscured with selfishness and pride. Let your face and your light from now on shine forth in and through all of us.

Thank you for all those who today are helping your most spurned brothers and sisters and also are helping you in them.

Jesus, I especially ask you to help my people get rid of the blasphemy with which so many defile your face and your name, your honor and your glory. Forgive and give new graces.

Mary, in your heart you thanked Veronica for her little favor to Jesus. Mary, obtain by prayer a great gift from your Son for me and for all pilgrims that his face may be reflected in our faces. This is your wish, too:

»**Dear children: Today I invite you to decide whether you are willing to live the messages I am giving you. I want you to be active in living and conveying the messages. Dear children, I especially want you to be a reflection of Jesus which will shine to this unbelieving world which is walking in darkness. I want you all to be a light to all and to testify in the light. Dear children, you are not invited to darkness, you are invited to light. So live the light with your life. Thank you for having responded to my call**« (June 5, 1986).

Our Father, Hail Mary, Glory be...
Have mercy on us, O Lord.
Have mercy on us.

The Seventh Station

Jesus, you fall a second time under the cross.

We adore you, O Christ, and we bless you;
Because by your Holy Cross, you have redeemed the world.

»But I am a worm, not a man; the scorn of men, despised by the people. All who see me scoff at me; they mock me with parted lips, they wag their heads: 'He relied on the Lord; let him deliver him, let him rescue him, if He loves him.'«... »I am like water poured out; all my bones are racked. My heart has become like wax melting away within my bosom. My throat is dried up like baked clay, my tongue cleaves to my jaws; to the dust of death you have brought me down. Indeed, many dogs surround me, a pack of evildoers closes in upon me...« (Ps 22:7-9; 15-17).

Jesus, after the comforting meetings with your Mother, with Simon and Veronica, there followed a new fall. Certainly, harder and more painful than the first one. Hatred and wantonness were all around you. The weaker they saw you, the more they raged, but you continued your suffering and your journey.

Thank you, O Jesus, for your journey, for your fall and for your rising again.

Forgive me my falls, forgive me my decisions which were so short-lived. So easily do I forget my own journey and destination, and remain in evil habits. Jesus, now I want to rise again and I promise to rise whenever I fall. Thank you for being patient with me.

At this second fall of yours, I pray for all those who have fallen and who have become disappointed in themselves and in your mercy. Help them to rise. Let there be no more people who get stuck in their sins and the troubles of life along their journey. Let new strength and a new will for a fresh start flow through every heart.

Jesus, I pray to you also for those who have started a new life here in Medugorje, but have experienced the power of passion and bad habits and have fallen again. Do not let them abide in sin. Let them accept their backsliding in humbleness and simplicity. Do not let anybody be tempted beyond their own power.

Thank you, Mary, for these apparitions on account of which many have risen because they felt your love. Let your appealing and comforting and encouraging word echo in my heart:

»Dear children: I invite you, the parish, to pray more during this time that still

remains until the anniversary. Let your prayer be a sign of devotion to God. Dear children, I know you are all tired: no, you do not know how to abandon yourselves to me. Abandon yourselves completely to me these days. Thank you for having responded to my call« (June 13, 1985).

Mary, I pray to you for this parish, for myself and for all pilgrims. Let there be no more fatigue, let love overwhelm every fatigue that we may again start walking with you.

> Our Father, Hail Mary, Glory be...
> Have mercy on us, O Lord.
> Have mercy on us.

The Eighth Station

> Jesus, you speak a word to the women of Jerusalem.
> We adore you, O Christ, and we bless you;
> Because by your Holy Cross, you have redeemed the world.

»I will pour out on the house of David and on the inhabitants of Jerusalem a spirit of grace and petition; and they shall look on him whom they have thrust through, and they shall mourn for him as one mourns for an only son, and they shall grieve over him as one grieves over a

first-born. On that day the mourning in Jerusalem shall be as great as the mourning of Hadadrimmon in the plain of Megiddo. And the land shall mourn, each family apart..« (Zec 12:10-12).

»A large crowd of people followed Jesus, including many women who mourned and lamented him. Jesus turned to them and said, "Daughters of Jerusalem, do not weep for me; weep instead for yourselves and for your children, for indeed, the days are coming when people will say, 'Blessed are the barren, the wombs that never bore and the breasts that never nursed.' At that time people will say to the mountains, 'Fall upon us.' and to the hills, 'Cover us'"« (Lk 23:27-30).

Jesus, gentle and humble of heart your passion did not make you either blind or deaf. You saw the women weeping for you and over you. You have never liked an insincere word. You, sufferer for all mankind, by your passion and cross you did not want to arouse shallow compassion but invited all to a deep change of life. Thank you.

Jesus, forgive me for having looked for consolation where I could not find it. So many times have I overheard the truth and out of self-love turned to flatteries and lies. I did not have enough strength to speak the truth with love. I deluded myself and others with my flattering words. Forgive my insincerity and my fear which have induced me not always to seek truth in love. Help me that from now on I will never look for false consolation, nor accept it nor give it to others. I want to live my life in truth with others, in your light.

Forgive parents, and all those who educate the young, for having often closed their eyes before truth and for not having known how to convey it to others. Forgive also your whole Church for having often sought superficial solutions with this world, forgetting the thoroughness of love and forgiveness.

Mary, thank you for your words which I remember in front of this station:

»Dear children: I would like to guide you, but you do not want to listen to my messages. Today I call you to listen to the messages and then you will be able to live all that God tells me to convey to you. Open to God, and God will act through you and give you everything you need. Thank you for having responded to my call« (July 25, 1985).

Our Father, Hail Mary, Glory be...
　Have mercy on us, O Lord.
Have mercy on us.

The Ninth Station

Jesus, you fall a third time under the cross.

We adore You, O Christ, and we bless You;

Because by Your Holy Cross, you have redeemed the world.

»Where would you yet be struck, you that rebel again and again? The whole head is sick, the whole heart faint. From the sole of the foot to the head there is no sound spot; wound and welt and gaping gash, not drained or bandaged, or eased with salve« (Is 1:5-6).

»But he was pierced for our offenses, crushed for our sins, upon him was the chastisement that makes us whole. By his stripes we were healed« (Is 53:5).

»The stone which the builders rejected has become the cornerstone. By the Lord has this been done« (Ps 118:22-23).

Jesus, what else can I think before this third fall? I fall on my knees and observe with my heart what is happening to you. You are crushed to the end. Even those who were taking you to the place of crucifixion certainly became impatient because of your falls, for they slowed down their plans. But you were patient both with yourself and with them. You forgave them, Jesus, and presented your wounds and bruises from the falls to the Father for us. Thank you.

Forgive me, Jesus, for having been impatient so many times with the small and the weak, while, at the same time, I feared the stronger, hesitating to support truth. Jesus, forgive me that my love has been weak so many times and has not dressed the wounds of others nor spared them from bruises. Therefore I pray to you for all those whose sins I have caused. Help them now.

I pray to you, Jesus, for all families crushed with the sins of parents, with quarrels between father and mother, with discord between children and parents, with doubts, blasphemy, alcoholism, and the killing of innocent life in a mother's bosom. Jesus, let them rise and take on a new way.

I also pray to you for the young people who have become addicted to drugs and alcohol. Here, before your heaviest fall, I pray to you for the heaviest addicts who come and ask for your help.

Jesus, become the cornerstone for all of us. Do not let us ever reject you so that our house may be safe. The world has rejected you in many things today. That is why many families break up and nations decay. O

Jesus, be the cornerstone for us so that we may walk uprightly with you.

Mary, you experienced this fall, too. A new sword of sorrow pierced your heart. You went on suffering and offering the falls for new risings of us all. Thank you, O Mary, for the words which I now gladly recall:

»Dear children: Today I wish to tell you that God wants to send you trials which you can overcome by prayer. God is testing you through daily chores. Now pray to withstand peacefully every trial. From everything through which God tests you come more open to God and approach Him with love. Thank you for having responded to my call« (August 22, 1985).

Our Father, Hail Mary, Glory be...
Have mercy on us, O Lord.
Have mercy on us.

The Tenth Station

Jesus, you are stripped of your garments and given sour wine to drink.
We adore you, O Christ, and we bless you;
Because of your Holy Cross, you have redeemed the world.

»When the soldiers had crucified Jesus, they took his clothes and divided them into four shares, a share for each soldier. They also took his tunic, but the tunic was seamless, woven in one piece from the top down« (Jn 19:23).

»Put to death whatever in your nature is rooted in earth: fornication, uncleanness, passion, evil desires, and that lust which is idolatry. These are the sins which provoke God's wrath. Your own conduct was once of this sort, when these sins were your very life. You must put that aside now; all the anger and quick temper, the malice, the insults, the foul language. Stop lying to one another. What you have done is put aside your old self with its past deeds and put on a new man, one who grows in knowledge as he is formed anew in the image of his Creator. Because you are God's chosen ones, holy and beloved, clothe yourselves with heartfelt mercy, with kindness, humility, meekness, and patience« (Col 3:5-10; 12).

»Let us cast off deeds of darkness and put on the armor of light. Let us live honorably as in daylight; not in carousing and drunkenness, not in sexual excess and lust, not in quarreling and jealously« (Rom 13:12-13).

Jesus, I am ashamed of what they did to you. They stripped you of your garments. You remained without clothes, naked. You, divine Word, through whom all things were made and splendidly arrayed, stand naked.

You allowed it in order to remove the curse of sin and death from us and to clothe us in the blessing of life and resurrection. Thank you.

Jesus, forgive me for having given in to passions, for having indulged in the lusts of the body to the detriment of my spirit and my soul. Forgive me for having considered the needs of my body more important than the needs of my spirit. Give me the grace of conversion. Let your grace change my old garments into new ones, so that from now on I may live according to the law of the spirit. Help me to put aside all vices; fornication, passion, greed, anger, wrath, and malice.

Jesus, I ask the same from you also for those who come here. Let them go back home renewed. Let the laws of the spirit overpower the laws of the body, that they may be the witnesses of the new life which you won by your passion and death. Let them all be clothed in the new garments of goodness.

Forgive every individual all the sins of impurity, fornication and every kind of wickedness. Jesus, thank you for my being able to ask for all this with a renewed hope.

Mary, I cannot even imagine let alone feel how you were feeling at this station. I join now in your feelings and I want you to teach me to live by the spirit. Thank you for the word you said:

»Dear children: I want to clothe you, day by day, in light, goodness, obedience and God's love that you may be more beautiful and more prepared for your Master with every day. Dear children: Listen to and live my messages. I want to guide you. Thank you for having responded to my call« (October 24, 1985).

Mary, thank you for not putting up with the nakedness caused by my sin and thank you for desiring to clothe me in beautiful garments.

> Our Father, Hail Mary, Glory be...
> Have mercy on us, O Lord.
> Have mercy on us.

The Eleventh Station

Jesus, you are nailed to the cross.

We adore you, O Christ, and we bless you; Because by your Holy Cross, you have redeemed the world.

»Indeed, many dogs surround me, a pack of evildoers closes in upon me; they have pierced my hands and my feet; I can count all my

bones. *They look on and gloat over me; they divide my garments among them, and for my vesture they cast lots* (Ps 22:17-19).

Even when you were dead in sin and your flesh was uncircumcised, God gave you new life in company with Christ. He pardoned all our sins. He canceled the bond that stood against us with all its claims, snatching it up and nailing it to the cross (Col2:13-14).

O Jesus, the cross, which you have carried and which has bruised your already wounded shoulders, now becomes your hard bed. What pains you suffered while they were nailing you to the cross, nobody will ever be able to express.

Jesus, you opened a new way of salvation when you did not respond to insults, when you did not seek revenge for what they had done to you. Thank you, sufferer of all sufferers. Your suffering redeemed us, because you loved in suffering and suffered in love.

Forgive me, Jesus, for having nailed others to the column of shame with my behavior, for having driven others down to fear and anxiety with my anger, for having so many times nailed up the door of my heart with my hatred, keeping others out. Redeem me from unjust desires and from evil habits which are crucifying me.

O Jesus, redeem the poor who are nailed to the crosses of poverty due to exploitation and the unjust behavior of the rich. Redeem all the children whom parents are crucifying with their behavior. Redeem us, Jesus, from every crucifixion and tension between the state and the people.

Help us to crucify every passion, every anger, and every pride so that peace and love, reconciliation and understanding may be born.

Mary, every blow echoed in your motherly heart. You endured it all. You remained upright. Thank you for loving me and for wanting to lead me to salvation. Mary, help me so that everything within me that crucifies me or that I crucify others with, may be destroyed, so that from now on I may be crucified only by love for others. Thank you for this word of yours:

»Dear children: Today, too, I invite you to open more to God that he may act through you. As much as you open, so much fruit you shall receive. I want to call you to prayer again. Thank you for having responded to my call« (March 6, 1986).

Our Father, Hail Mary, Glory be...
Have mercy on us, O Lord.
Have mercy on us.

The Twelfth Station

Jesus, you die on the cross.
We adore you, O Christ, and we bless you;
Because by your Holy Cross, you have redeemed the world.

»If God is for us, who can be against us? Is it possible that he who did not spare his own Son but handed him over for the sake of us all will not grant us all things besides?« (Rom 8:31).

»It was for this you were called, since Christ suffered for you in just this way and left you an example, to have you follow in his footsteps. He did no wrong; no deceit was found in his mouth. When he was insulted, he returned no insult. When he was made to suffer, he did not counter with threats. Instead, he delivered himself up to the one who judges justly. In his own body he brought your own sins to the cross, so that all of us, dead to sin, could live in accord with God's will. By his wounds you were healed. At one time you were straying like sheep, but now you have returned to the shepherd, the guardian of your souls« (1Pt 2:21-25).

»...he humbled himself, becoming obedient to death, even to death on a cross« (Phil 2:8).

»Near the cross of Jesus there stood his mother Mary« (Jn 19:25).

My Jesus, look where love for us and obedience to the Father has brought you. Who of us will ever fathom your love? So thank you for having loved us so much that we cannot even understand it. Let your pierced heart be salvation for us all.

I want to be an answer to your love. I kneel before your cross, and want to hear and to listen to your word with love. Let it enter into my heart as it did into the heart of your Mother Mary who had strength enough to stand by your cross.

(Remain in silence.)

Heavenly Father, thank you for having entrusted your Son Jesus Christ with such a commission. Thank you for his having accomplished it even unto his death on the cross. Thank you for having accepted his prayer to forgive us.

I also forgive all those who have insulted me. I pray to you for all those who do not forgive yet. Let your mercy and the suffering of your Son stir them to forgive so that peace may come to all men.

Mary, it was not easy for you to understand the Father's will, but you accepted it along with your Son. Thank you for having accepted us as your children. John, thank you for having accepted Mary in the name of all of us, and for having in that way expressed to her gratitude in our name. And thank you, Mary, for the next call:

»**Dear children: I want to tell you that the cross is central these days. Pray especially before the cross, from which great graces come. Now make a special devotion to the cross in your homes. Promise that you will not offend Jesus or the cross and inflict insults on him. Thank you for having responded to my call«** (September 12, 1985).

Our Father, Hail Mary, Glory be...
Have mercy on us, O Lord.
Have mercy on us.

The Thirteenth Station

Jesus, you are taken from the cross and laid in your Mother's arms.
We adore you, O Christ, and we bless you;
Because by your Holy Cross, you have redeemed the world.

»*There was a man named Joseph, an upright and holy member of the Sanhedrin, who had not been associated with their plan or*

*their action. He was from Arimathea, a Jewish
town, and he looked expectantly for the reign
of God. This man approached Pilate with a
request for Jesus' body. He took it down,
wrapped it in fine linen, and laid it in a tomb
hewn out of the rock, in which no one had yet
been buried« (Lk 23:50-54).*

Jesus, you ended your life on earth in
terrible suffering. You died as a hero of love
and forgiveness. You commended your
spirit into the Father's hands. You took the
criminal on the cross to heaven with you
because he asked you to remember him.
Jesus, thank you for your coming to us,
thank you for every word, for every deed, for
every sign by which you showed that you
love us.

Mary, you stood at the foot of the Cross.
You heard everything, and you suffered
everything and now you are holding your
Son in your motherly lap, before his burial.
With how much love and tenderness you
took him from the Cross! No one shall ever
be able either to understand or to describe
that moment. Mary, thank you for your
warm motherly lap. Thank you for having
taken him in your arms at the presentation
and for having carried him in your bosom.

Thank you for the Son of God's having
become man and our Savior in your bosom.

Thank you for receiving him in your arms even after men had killed him by nailing him to the Cross. Thank you for your having committed him back to the earth with hope and faith.

Mary, now through you I ask for forgiveness of every sin which brought coldness into my heart, spreading ice and chill all around. Thank you for being ready to take me into your motherly arms to comfort me and lead me further on the way to the Lord.

Mary, I pray to you for all your children throughout the world, especially for those who have grown cold, or whom sin has killed long ago, so that they are now in the grip of death menaced by eternal death. Take them down from their crosses and let them come back to life by the power of God's Spirit.

Mary, I pray to you especially for abandoned children who do not know the warmth of a mother's lap. Please be a mother to them, give them back the will to live. Mary, I pray to you for the mothers whose bosoms have become the graveyards of life, for they have either killed or abandoned their children. Restore them to life, too. Let the mother's bosom revive and do not let any become the grave but rather the cradle of life. Mary, thank you for the following words:

»Dear children: I have already told you that I have chosen you in a special way, just the way you are. I, the Mother, love you all. So have no fear of hard moments, because I love you even when you are far from me and my Son. I beg you, do not let my heart weep bloody tears because of the souls who perish in sin. Therefore, dear children, pray, and pray, and pray. Thank you for having responded to my call« (May 24, 1984).

> Mary, from now on I shall present you prayers for the salvation of all.
> Our Father, Hail Mary, Glory be...
> Have mercy on us, O Lord.
> Have mercy on us.

The Fourteenth Station

> Jesus, you are laid in the sepulcher.
> We adore you, O Christ, and we bless you;
> Because by your Holy Cross, you have redeemed the world.

»A grave was assigned him among the wicked, and a burial place with evildoers, though he had done no wrong nor spoken any falsehood« (Is 53:9).

201

»And my body rests in peace and hope, carefree; because you will not abandon me to the nether world, nor will you suffer the Holy One of God to undergo decay and corruption. You will show me the path to life, fullness of joys in your presence, that delights at your right hand forever« (Cf Ps 16:9-11).

»In baptism you were not only buried with him but also raised to life with him because you believed in the power of God who raised him from the dead« (Col 2:12).

»When the corruptible frame takes on incorruptibility and the mortal, immortality, then will the saying of Scripture be fulfilled. 'O death, where is your victory? O death, where is your sting.'... But thanks be to God who has given us the victory through our Lord Jesus Christ« (1 Cor 15:54-57).

Jesus, you accepted the cross and death, and the tomb that you may be equal to us. By your cross you consecrated suffering, by your death you destroyed death, and by your tomb you opened all tombs. Thank you. While I am standing over your tomb, I am also thinking about my life and my end. I know neither the day nor the hour. But now again I give my life and my death over to you. I give over to you my fear of death, too. Let the moment of my passing away be consecrated by your presence. Give me the consciousness that I always live in the light of this passage so that nothing in this world can stop or obstruct me on the way to you. Grant that I may find rest in the Father's bosom forever.

I pray to you now for those who are dying a natural death, prepared. I also pray for those who are dying a sudden death, especially a violent one, who are dying embittered and desperate. I pray to you for all those who find themselves with the dying. Let their presence be a help to them in death's hour. I also pray to you for those who are dying in an inhumane way. Be close to them and take them into your heaven. Save us all from eternal darkness. Bring us into your light which shone forth over your tomb on the third day.

Mary, be with me at the hour of my death. Take my life into your motherly lap. Mary, let me understand all that you have offered me here and live in joyful seriousness with you so that from now on I may do the Father's will everyday as you did. Let every evil die within me and the good and rise to new life.

Thank you for this call:

»Dear children: Today also I want to call you to accept and follow the messages I give you with all seriousness. Dear child-

ren, it is because of you that I have stayed so long in order to help you realize all the messages I give you. Therefore, dear children, follow all the messages I give you out of love for me. Thank you for having responded to my call« (October 30, 1986).

Our Father, Hail Mary, Glory be...
Have mercy on us, O Lord.
Have mercy on us.

PRAYER ON THE SITE OF APPARITIONS

Mary, here I am, on your Podbrdo. Here I am, on the spot where the eyes of your chosen ones first saw you. Here I am, O Lady, on the spot where you chose to start the great renewal of your children. Here I am, Mother of love, on the spot which you filled with your presence. Here I am, Mother of Peace, on the spot from where you, with a big cross in your hands, called everybody through tears, to peace and reconciliation. I have come to be with you in this place. I want to say my »thank you« to you here on this rocky ground, in silence and solitude.

Thank you, Mother, for having come to us. Thank you for your special preference for the simple, the small and the lowly. Thank you for your motherly love and care that you show to us. Thank you for the hope and joy you give us by your coming. Thank you for sharing our joy.

»Dear children: I thank the Lord again today for everything He gives to me, especially for this gift that I can be with you today, too. Dear children, these are the days when the Father is giving special graces to all who open their heart. I bless you and I want you, too, dear children, to recognize the graces and to put yourselves at God's disposal that He may be glorified through you. My heart carefully watches your steps. Thank you for having responded to my call« (December 25, 1986).

Mary, thank you for having opened so many hearts and souls with your motherly love, that they may put themselves at the disposal of God, as you did.

Heavenly Father, I join Mary in saying to you, »Here I am, I am ready to do your will.« That is not difficult for me on account of the love and peace I feel here now. I open to your word as the eyes of the visionaries opened at the moment of their gracious meeting with your faithful servant and our Mother.

Father, allow her to touch my life and my heart now again as she touched these rocks, brambles and thorn bushes. My heart is often as hard as stone and as prickly as brambles. Father, allow Our Lady to take me into her arms as she, on the second day of apparitions, held a child in her arms, showing it to the visionaries from afar. Life has buffeted me all over. Let me find healing and appeasement in her bosom today again.

Mary, thank you for the experience of the visionaries on the second day of your apparitions. They were able to fly up here without having felt rocks or brambles. They were running to you and nobody could catch up with them. Our dear Lady, look how my step falters, how many times I am tired and burdened and cannot budge. I get stuck in trials too often and do not move on. My heart and my eyes are turned to the rocks and the brambles of life so that I cannot see a way through, and even if I start, I soon get tired and cut up. Today I have climbed your hill. I did not come flying up like the visionaries did. But just because of that, I all the more heartily ask you in this blessed place to make my steps through this world easier with your blessing. I put myself, in all my weakness caused by sin and evil, at your disposal. Mary, thank you for every time you have come by which you joined us all.

I pray to you also for all those who are still far away, who have fallen behind on the way, tired. Let them all feel the joy of your comings as you are happy about each of us. Let them move. Let them be reconciled and overcome all the rocky ground of life and find new ways of togetherness.

I pray to you, Mary, for the whole world, for all the persons in places of authority in all nations and states. Direct their hearts to peace. Bless them, too, that they may know how to bring others to the way of peace.

O good Mother, I want my heart to become totally obedient like yours, and cleansed, as yours has been since your Immaculate Conception. I also want to be in the light from now on, wrapped in the cloak of love and safety. I want, like you, to have every evil and sin under my feet. I want to crush the head of Satan. Mary, I want to be completely yours. Thank you for having said that you want to transform my heart, too, and to conform it to your motherly heart. I want to return home that way to other people, to my family, and to the world.

And now I remain silent. I only want to feel your love and presence with my heart and soul. Leaning against a rock, I want to listen to the beats of my heart, as if I were in your bosom. Appease my heart so that peace may enter into it. Bless me, Mother. Amen.

PRAYER BEFORE MASS

Heavenly Father, I give you thanks that I need encounters with you and with men. Thank you for creating me for togetherness and that the love of others makes me happy. Thank you for every friendly hand which helps me go through this life. Thank you for all the encounters in which I have felt that others are happy with me and in which I have brought joy to others.

I give you special thanks for having made today's meeting with your Son, Jesus Christ, possible for me; your Son who has remained for me in his holy Word and in the Eucharist, the Sacred Host. Thank you for his presence among us.

Jesus, I am eager to meet you in this Holy Mass. I am eager to hear your Word. I am eager to receive you in the Sacred Host. You are my friend. I dare to come to you even when others despise me. Only you can appease my heart. Send me your Spirit that I may understand what it means to live with you.

Mary, Mother, you lived with Jesus every day for such a long time and so you know him best. Help me to remove everything that is in the way of my meeting with him. Mary, thank you for having invited me to prepare for Mass like one prepares for a meeting with a friend.

»Dear children: I would like to invite you to live holy Mass. There are a lot of you who have felt the beauty of Holy Mass, but there are also others who come unwillingly. I have chosen you, dear children, and Jesus bestows upon you his graces in Mass. Therefore, live consciously Holy Mass and let your coming be a joyful one. Come and accept Holy Mass with love. Thank you for having responded to my call« (April 3, 1986).

Mary, I want to live in the love which will be offered to me in this Mass, too. Obtain by prayer the grace for me that the Word of your Son may move me, that his love may incite me to love, that his forgiveness may enable me to forgive. Let me be happy with the every Mass I participate in, just as you were happy over every meeting with your Son.

Jesus, remove all the burdens and loads from me that this Mass may be a spring of joy for my having met you. Thank you, Jesus, for your wish to meet me, too.

Jesus, forgive me for not having thought of you during Mass so many times because I was burdened with other meetings and things. Therefore, the meeting with you was without joy. Sometimes I did not know why I was there but you presented yourself on the altar with undiminished love. Forgive me and take away my burdens so that this Mass may now be a real meeting with you.

Jesus, I pray to you also for the priest who is going to celebrate this Mass. Let his heart be ready to forgive everybody. Remove any burdens from his heart for this sacrifice and communion. Help him to overcome the habit and routine of celebrating Mass. Let every Mass be a meeting for him on which he will live and which he will readily make possible for others. I pray to you for the priests who are caught up in everyday worries and have no time to prepare for Holy Mass. Jesus, fill their hearts to proclaim your Word with joy; a joy which they have experienced in their own hearts.

(Pray with your own words mentioning the name of the priest.)

Jesus, I know how many could be here now at this Holy Mass. But many have stopped coming because of material worries and running after money, because they have broken off with you. Jesus, I can understand you if you are sad. You come, you sacrifice yourself and offer yourself as food and drink but they remain far away, hungry, thirsty and tired. Jesus, I beseech you to send them grace that they may hear your call, respond to it and come prepared for your coming.

I pray to you for the young, too, whom you also want to meet. They also long for a meeting with you in Holy Mass but do not come, and if they do, they do not know how to respond and are bored. Open their hearts also to the mystery of this communion so that they may enjoy it.

Here, while I am preparing for this communion with you, I recommend to you all my friends and acquaintances, especially the sick and the old who are not able to come any longer. Jesus, let them meet you in those who have attended the Mass. I present them all to you and come to this Mass in their name.

(Mention the names of the sick.)

Jesus, I also pray to you for the acolytes, the musicians, the singers and readers. Let them serve the altar with joy, let them sing joyfully and proclaim your Word. Let our hearts join in song and be attentive, listening. Let everything leap with joy because you are coming, you who are blessed forever. Let love fill all hearts, and sin and hatred disappear, that everything may burst into flower, for you give yourself for us with all love. O, grant that I may understand the mystery of your sacrifice for us and profoundly bow before you with all creatures and the whole of heaven.

Jesus, let the love in my family, in my community and in the whole world grow stronger with this Mass.

Jesus, everything in my heart is ready for this meeting with you. Let all who are here with me now also be ready. Let every soul be clothed in the whiteness of joy. Let every sin and its consequences disappear, that you may also be happy with us. Come, Jesus, I am awaiting you. My longing for you has become deeper. Thank you for coming. Let this Holy Mass begin in your name. Amen.

THANKSGIVING AFTER HOLY MASS

Jesus, after this joyful meeting with you, send me out into the world again. You give me your blessing and you do not leave me alone. You want me to bear the peace and love I have received here from you. Here I am, Jesus, I am ready to testify to you. Bless me. Bless also those I am going to live and work with today.

Jesus, you said that we are the light of the world. Let your light kindle in my heart and grow so strong that no gale or storm, no passion or sin may ever extinguish it. With the light that I have received from you I want to inflame new lights, that there may be no darkness in relationships among people any more.

Jesus, you have offered yourself to me in this Mass as the Way. Help me never to leave your way and to follow it ever more steadily. I especially pray to you, on my way to the cross. Make my patience stronger than impatience, my peace stronger than unrest, my love stronger than hatred.

Jesus, today you want to make use of my steps to be a friend and a guest to the sick and the weak. Here, bless my steps. Let these become the steps of peace and reconciliation, the steps by which you will be closer today to all who are lonely.

Jesus, I know that today you want to act through my hands. Consecrate and bless my hands that they may never reach out for evil or stretch a finger of accusation against others.

Jesus, with your eyes you warned, expressed sympathy and called to love. Love and peace, mercy and righteousness glowed in your eyes. I consecrate my eyes to you today. Bless them that they may never be dimmed with the sin of selfishness and haughtiness. Let them never become eyes that boil with hatred and vengeance.

Jesus, your heart beat for all men and brought warmth to everybody. Make my heart like unto your heart now, so that through my heart, love may enter into my family and come to the people I live with. Through my heart, Jesus, find also the sick that they may feel your love. Make my heart like unto yours that it may have more understanding for everybody.

Mary, you are my Mother. After meeting your Son in this Mass I want to go into life with you. Obtain by prayer for me the grace of testifying and conveying love as you called me:

»Dear children: Today I call you to decide whether you want to live the messages I give you. I want you to be active in living and conveying the messages. Especially, dear children, I want you all to be a reflection of Jesus which will shine to this unbelieving world walking in darkness. I want you all to be the light to everybody and to testify in the light. Dear children, you are not called to darkness but to the light. Therefore, live the light with your life. Thank you for having responded to my call« (June 5, 1986).

Mary, your wishes are my commands. Thank you for the promised help and for the confidence in sending me to others. Let the Father's will be done in me and through me. Amen.

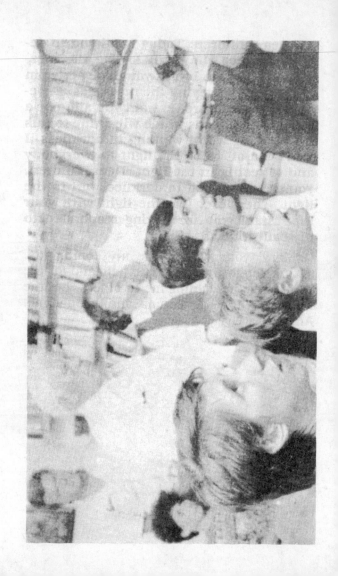

PRAYERS FOR HEALING

(Prayers for healing are prayed in Medugorje after the evening Mass. Prayers similar to the following may be prayed elsewhere according to circumstances.)

Jesus, you came because of the sick and the sinful. Therefore, I turn to you and want to ask you to heal my soul and body. You know, Jesus, that sin tears and rips up the whole human being and that it destroys relations between people and with you. But there is no sin and no illness that you cannot drive away with your Almighty Word. There is no wound you cannot heal.

Mary, you called me to pray for healing. I want to do it now. So I ask you to accompany my prayer with your faith. Pray with me now that I may be worthy of obtaining by prayer the graces for me personally and for others who are sick and infirm.

1. Come, O Lord!

»He got into the boat and his disciples followed him. Without warning a violent storm came up on the sea, and the boat began to be swamped by the waves. Jesus was sleeping soundly, so they made their way toward him and woke him, 'Where is your courage? How little faith you have.' Then he stood up and took the winds and the sea to task. Complete calm

219

ensued; the men were dumbfounded. 'What sort of man is this', they said, 'that even the winds and the sea obey him?'« (Mt 8:23-24)

Jesus, you entered into the storms of the world. You also get into the boat of every life. You are present, for your name is Emmanuel, God with us, God for us. So I am asking you now to come into my life. The boat of my life also begins to be swamped, in my consciousness and in my subconsciousness. Enter, Jesus, into the depths of my soul. I am lost. Stand up and tell my unrest to calm down, tell the death waves which surround me to stop threatening. Say the word to appease my heart that it may be able to hear your divine, creative Word.

(Remain in silence.)

Come, Jesus, into the boat of my family and of the whole world, as well. Let our cries wake you up. Stretch out your hand that calm may follow. Come, O Lord Jesus, come. Come to where I am most wounded. (Mention any areas where you know you are wounded and need to be healed.)

Come, Jesus, also into those boats of life which stand anchored to bad habits, to drugs, to alcohol, to bodily pleasures, and who do not move forward. Jesus, calm the storms. Let everybody hear your voice which brings peace.

2. Decision

Jesus, you are in my boat of life. You are my God, I adore you, I glorify you, for you alone are the Holy One, you alone are the Lord. I believe in you and I put everything at your disposal with trust. I decide for your love and your mercy. With you and your Mother I say: »Let your will be done to me in health and in sickness, in success and in failure, in joys and sorrows, in life and in death, in the present and in eternity.«

Jesus, I have often been indecisive for the good, I have often done my will and so got slashed all over. Cure me of my unbelief and the resistance which I have offered when I failed to understand the Father's will.

Mary, obtain by prayer the grace for me that my decision may be a final one. Help me never to revoke it but to remain faithful.

(Silence)

3. Renunciation

Jesus, I renounce every sin. I renounce Satan, and all his seductions, his lies and promises. I renounce every idol and all idolatry. I renounce my unforgiveness and hatred, my selfishness and haughty life. I

221

give up all the desires which have caused me to forget the Father's will. I give up every spiritual illness and neglect so that you, Jesus, may enter into my soul.

Mary, Mother, help me crush Satan's head in my life.

4. Prayer for Love

»*You have heard the commandment, 'You shall love your countryman but hate your enemy.' My command to you is: Love your enemies, pray for your persecutors. This will prove that you are sons of your heavenly Father...*« (Mt 5:43-44).

Jesus, you called me to love. I admit to you that my love is weak. Cure me of the wounds resulting from the lack of love, and of all the sins that prevent me from loving you above all, O my God. Cure my heart of the painful heritage I brought to this world because of the sins of the world and of my parents. Cure my soul of all the burdens which have accumulated in me through my childhood and youth.

Let the fire of love, kindled by the grace of healing, destroy every darkness and completely melt the ice of evil in me. Enable me to love completely that I may love all men with my whole heart, even those who have insulted me. So often, Jesus, have I felt the inability of my love to forgive insults. Forgive my envy and jealously that I use to burden myself and others with.

Heal my faith in you, too. Let the grace of trust remove every mistrust and every source of fear. Cure me of the godlessness in my thoughts, in my words, in my deeds.

Jesus, heal love in my family, too, so that it may be as it was in yours. Heal love between spouses, between children and parents, between the sick and the healthy.

Jesus, heal love for all men throughout the world.

(Silence. Pray in silence for the person whom, at the hour of prayer, you do not love or whom you have not forgiven.)

5. Prayer for Healing of the Soul

Jesus, now I thank you for my soul, too.

All the consequences of sin reflect themselves in my soul, too. That is why I am often nervous and aggressive. I am often impatient and revengeful. Bad habits have settled in my soul, wounds and scars have remained, which make my love of others more difficult. Certain experiences have settled to the bottom, often making me distrustful.

Jesus, cleanse my subconscious. Enter with your light into my subconscious that darkness may never overwhelm it. With the power of your grace touch those layers of my soul, too, in which the addictions to material things, which breed fear, have settled. Cleanse me that my spirit may be more open to you.

Heal me of mistrust in you and in your Word. Jesus, I beg you, heal me of all wounds and frustrations caused by failures and unfulfilled wishes. Cure me of every inner darkness and heal the wounds in the depths of my subconscious being. Let my subconscious calm down in you, Jesus.

Now I pray to you also for all who are mentally ill and encumbered. Take off their burdens and clean the wounds which develop into mental diseases. Help the children who have inherited heavy mental burdens. Cure every split personality, all depression and fear, every neurosis and psychopathic state.

Cure also all those who have become mentally ill due to a failure in the family, at school or at work. Remove from them the thoughts of suicide and free them from every forced thought.

Jesus, be the Master of our souls. Cure all who have busied themselves with suspicious practices. Deliver them from every consequence of witchcraft and sorcery. Rest every soul and restore peace to it.

6. Prayer for Physical Healing

»As evening drew on, they brought him many who were possessed. He expelled the spirits by a simple command and cured all who were afflicted, thereby fulfilling what had been said through Isaiah the prophet, 'It was our infirmities he bore, our sufferings he endured'« (Mt 8:16-17).

Jesus, cure my body. Here I am before you with my physical pains and the dangers threatening my body. Cure me of the diseases which are affecting my body now.

(Mention your own disease.)

Protect me from every disease.

If it is your will for me to carry the cross of illness, then I accept the cross and ask you for the grace to carry it with love. Jesus, now I pray to you for the healing of the members of my family and my relatives.

(Mention their names here.)

Jesus, I pray to you, if it is the Father's will for them to suffer, give them the strength to bear their crosses with love.

Cure all the sick in the world. Protect the world from epidemics and incurable diseases. Jesus, in one word, cure all our illnesses, for you came to take them upon yourself and to save us.

Heavenly Father, thank you for having created me, for having redeemed me through your Son. Thank you for healing my body, my soul and my love through him now. Let the blessing of peace and reconciliation, of love and trust pour out on me, on my family, on the whole Church and on the whole world. Let Mary, our Mother, obtain from your fatherly goodness, by praying together with us, all that we need for soul and body.

May it be so. Amen.

WHEN YOU RETURN HOME

Dear pilgrim, seeker of God, when you come to Medugorje, you are called to pray in the church, to celebrate the Mass, to confess, to adore Jesus in the Most Holy Sacrament of the Altar, to pray on Križevac (the hill which reminds us of the passion and death of Christ as well as of our own suffering and our own cross) and on Podbrdo, the Hill of Apparitions. I believe that you have done that, that you have renewed your faith, love and hope and that you have felt how near God is. Anyway, that is exactly the reason for your coming here.

And really, God is very close here to all who are seeking Him. You can feel His presence, you can come to love Him. He gives us the strength to abandon ourselves to Him. God has created here an oasis of PEACE through the Queen of Peace.

I am sure that there is a question now on your lips which bothers many pilgrims. It is nice here. It is easy here. Everybody is praying, everybody is seeking God. But at home? What can I do there for my peace to grow, for my love to develop? What can I do so that trust may overcome mistrust, that the spirit of reconciliation may be stronger than unreconciliation? This question is of decisive importance.

Međugorje is what Tabor was for the disciples: to convince us that it is possible to live love and to experience the glory of God. But then one has to return home, to one's own Jerusalem, to one's own everyday routine, to work, to school, among people who do not have the same conviction.

Yes, one has to return home.

In Međugorje you prayed for long hours. It was not difficult for you to climb Križevac no matter if the weather was good or bad. You also found time for Podbrdo. And you were fine.

Now leave Međugorje as a parish community and go back home. In your heart take along the places and events of Međugorje.

We know one thing: at home you have your own Križevac, your own hill of the cross, your own cross and suffering. You left it at home and it is waiting for you. But have no fear. The Križevac of Međugorje is not easier than your own back home. Nevertheless, the cross at home has become understandable and bearable for many, since the lower hill, the Hill of Apparitions, became, by God's Will, a place of intensive communion with God through Mary. Therefore, although your Križevac at home, often built out of troubles and sufferings for which you are neither responsible nor to blame, is standing and waiting for you, build a smaller hill next to it right away, build your own Hill of Apparitions, your own Tabor.

Then your Križevac, too, will get a new color, will be wrapped up in new peace and new hope. Build the Hill of Apparitions in one corner of your apartment or house. Furnish it with a small crucifix, a candle, the Bible, rosary beads and a kneeler. There you will understand your Križevac, too, and your passage, and your passing. By the side of the Hill of Apparitions, Križevac becomes a place of resurrection, for no Križevac is there to destroy you, but to help you attain to salvation.

Remember well that Our Lady has taken Christ's words seriously. She goes with you up to your Križevac, up to your Calvary, as she said in a message of Christmas 1986:

»Dear children: Today also I give thanks to the Lord for all that He is doing for me, especially for this gift that I am able to be with you also today. Dear children, there are the days in which the Father grants special graces to all who

229

open their hearts. I bless you and I desire that you too, dear children, become alive to the graces and place everything at God's disposal so that He may be glorified through you. My heart carefully follows your progress. Thank you for having responded to my call« (December 25, 1986).

This message does not refer only to those who are in Medugorje or only to the visionaries. It is addressed to me, to you, to everybody.

Go home, blessed forever by the Forever Blessed, and build an altar on which you start to offer your crosses and pains, woes and troubles, hopes and joys, love and faith everyday. Thus you will have your church, and your Križevac, and your Podbrdo. Thus God will be with you, and Mary will carefully watch your steps.

Go in peace. Bear peace and blessing.

Together with Mary give thanks to the Lord for the great things that He does within you.

Magnificat

My soul proclaims the greatness of the Lord,
My spirit rejoices in God my Savior;
For He has looked with favor on His lowly
    servant,
      And from this day all generations will call
        me blessed.
The Almighty has done great things for me:
Holy is His Name.
He has mercy on those who fear Him in every
    generation.
He has shown the strength of His arm,
He has scattered the proud in their conceit.
He has cast down the mighty from their
    thrones,
      And has lifted up the lowly.
He has filled the hungry with good things,
      And has sent the rich away empty.
He has come to the help of His servant Israel
      For He has remembered His promise of
        mercy,
The promise He made to our fathers,
      To Abraham and his children forever.

Međugorje Hymn

1. We come to you Dear Mother,
from all parts of the world;
we bring you our problems
and with them our desires.

Chorus: Look on us, console us,
Lay your hands upon us;
Intercede for us to your Son.
Mother of Peace, pray for us.

2. The whole church looks to you,
the last star of salvation;
purify us, embrace us,
with all our hearts we pray you.

3. Your little Bijakovo
and all Međugorje,
together spread your glory
and exult your name.

4. For all the love dear Mother
you have poured out to us here,
we promise you in the future
to be better than we were.

In the name of the Father, and of the Son, and of the Holy Spirit. Amen.
The Apostles' Creed

I believe in God, the Father almighty,
>creator of heaven and earth.

I believe in Jesus Christ, his only Son, our Lord,

Who was conceived by the power of the Holy Spirit,
>born of the Virgin Mary,
>suffered under Pontius Pilate,
>was crucified, died, and was buried.

He descended to the dead.

On the third day he rose again.

He ascended into heaven,
>and is seated at the right hand of the Father.

He will come again to judge
>the living and the dead.

I believe in the Holy Spirit,
>the holy Catholic Church,
>the communion of saints,
>the forgiveness of sins,
>the resurrection of the body,
>and the life everlasting. Amen.

Our Father

Our Father, who art in heaven
hallowed be thy name;
Thy kingdom come;
thy will be done on earth
as it is in heaven.
Give us this day our daily bread;
and forgive us our trespasses
as we forgive those
who trespass against us;
And lead us not into temptation,
but deliver us from evil. Amen.

Hail Mary

Hail Mary, full of grace.
The Lord is with you.
Blessed are you among women,
and blessed is the fruit
of your womb, Jesus.
Holy Mary, Mother of God,
pray for us sinners,
Now and at the hour of our death. Amen.

Glory Be

Glory be to the Father, and to the Son,
and to the Holy Spirit.
As it was in the beginning, is now,
and ever shall be;
World without end. Amen.

O My Jesus

Oh my Jesus, forgive us our sins,
  save us from the fire of hell.
Lead all souls to heaven,
  especially those who have most need
  of Thy mercy.

Međugorje